Toward Incentives for Military Transformation

A Review of Economic Models of Compensation

Bogdan Savych

Prepared for the Office of the Secretary of Defense

NATIONAL DEFENSE RESEARCH INSTITUTE

The research described in this report was sponsored by the Office of the Secretary of Defense (OSD). The research was conducted in the RAND National Defense Research Institute, a federally funded research and development center supported by the OSD, the Joint Staff, the unified commands, and the defense agencies under Contract DASW01-01-C-0004.

Library of Congress Cataloging-in-Publication Data

Savych, Bogdan.
    Toward incentives for military transformation : a review of economic models of compensation /
Bogdan Savych.
        p. cm.
    "TR-194."
    Includes bibliographical references.
    ISBN 0-8330-3786-2 (pbk.)
        1. United States—Armed Forces—Pay, allowances, etc. 2. United States—Armed Forces—Reorganization.
    I. Title.

UC74.S28 2005
355'.00973'0905—dc22

                                                                        2005008170

The RAND Corporation is a nonprofit research organization providing objective analysis and effective solutions that address the challenges facing the public and private sectors around the world. RAND's publications do not necessarily reflect the opinions of its research clients and sponsors.

RAND˚ is a registered trademark.

Published 2005 by the RAND Corporation
1776 Main Street, P.O. Box 2138, Santa Monica, CA 90407-2138
1200 South Hayes Street, Arlington, VA 22202-5050
201 North Craig Street, Suite 202, Pittsburgh, PA 15213-1516
RAND URL: http://www.rand.org/
To order RAND documents or to obtain additional information, contact
Distribution Services: Telephone: (310) 451-7002;
Fax: (310) 451-6915; Email: order@rand.org

PREFACE

Recent efforts toward military transformation have extensive implications for the military's personnel management and compensation systems. In addition to the existing goals of ensuring effective participation of individuals in the military (attracting, retaining, and developing qualified personnel), the compensation and personnel systems of a transformed military should emphasize effort and performance incentives by encouraging reasonable risk-taking and innovation, allow for greater speed and flexibility in deployment, and support more decentralized forces. The worry, however, is that current military systems cannot facilitate simultaneously all the needs of a transformed military.

This report reviews economic models of compensation in a hierarchical organization and identifies factors within the military compensation system that might constrain or facilitate transformation efforts. In particular, it focuses on how lessons from these economic compensation models can be used to increase flexibility of personnel management and provide incentives for creative thinking and performance and well-calculated risk-taking. Frameworks reviewed in this report are useful in describing the behavior of military personnel and patterns of performance in the military. This report is part of a larger project titled "Enhancing the Flexibility of the Military Compensation System." The project seeks to define ways of simplifying and adding flexibility to the military compensation system that bring value to the military organization and support the goals of military transformation. Further effort within the project would use existing military compensation models to determine what changes to the compensation system would support transformation.

This research was conducted for the Office of Compensation, Office of the Under Secretary of Defense for Personnel and Readiness, within the Forces and Resources Policy Center of the RAND National Defense Research Institute (NDRI). NDRI, a division of the RAND Corporation, is a federally funded research and development center sponsored by the

Office of the Secretary of Defense, the Joint Staff, the unified commands, and the defense agencies. Comments are welcome and may be addressed to the project leaders, Beth Asch, beth_asch@rand.org, and James Hosek, james_hosek@rand.org. For more information on RAND's Forces and Resources Policy Center, contact the Director, Susan Everingham. She can be reached by email at susan_everingham@rand.org; by phone at 310-393-0411, extension 7654; or by mail at RAND Corporation, 1776 Main Street, P.O. Box 2138, Santa Monica, California 90401-2138. More information about RAND is available at www.rand.org.

CONTENTS

SUMMARY

This report reviews economic models of compensation that apply to hierarchical organizations. It outlines how models of compensation can help make the military compensation system more compatible with the goals of transformation. Two objectives of transformation are important here: (1) assuring that the compensation system provides flexibility in managing personnel, and (2) assuring that the system induces innovatory activities and well-calculated risk-taking. These aims should accompany the usual goals of the military compensation system in providing incentives for performance, retention, and skill acquisition.

This report is organized around four main paradigms of personnel compensation. First, it discusses the advantages and disadvantages of providing incentives through promotion tournaments. This is the most important model of compensation in the military. Next, it examines how incentives are provided in compensation systems that defer some part of the rewards into the future. This analytical approach to compensation applies to the military because performance in the military in the current period is partially rewarded by higher pay in the future through promotions and eventually retirement. The report also looks at the benefits and costs of tying pay directly to certain performance metrics. This approach provides the most flexibility in personnel management and can provide strong incentives for individual performance. However, its application in the military is limited to those occupations where performance is easy to measure. In addition, the report outlines how nonmonetary factors can affect performance and sorting in the organization, and how they should be associated with monetary incentives.

Each of these models of rewarding personnel has its benefits. A well-designed compensation system can ensure that workers with the right skills and abilities apply for open positions in an organization and stay there for their careers. When deciding where to work and later whether to separate from a firm, workers consider the compensation that they receive and compare it to the opportunities available elsewhere. In addition, a compensation system can ensure that employees work hard on their jobs.

However, each of the systems of rewarding personnel has its costs. Monetary costs of rewarding personnel include wages, costs of monitoring performance, and possible administrative expenses. More important, reward systems might create unintended outcomes, brought about by the strategic response of personnel to the peculiarities of the compensation system. Some of these unintended outcomes include the following:

- Workers may inefficiently allocate their efforts among different tasks. If not all dimensions of the output are rewarded, workers may prefer to work harder only in measured and rewarded dimensions at the expense of unmeasured and unrewarded ones.
- Incentive systems can affect workers' risk-taking behavior. Workers can either take excessive risks or limit their risk-taking too much.
- Workers may strategically shift their effort between measurement periods.
- Workers may prefer to influence supervisors' evaluations. When performance evaluations include subjective components, workers may invest too much of their time into affecting the supervisors' evaluations, because good evaluations affect future pay and workers' reputations.
- Supervisors may rely on favoritism or preferences in deciding whom to promote. This makes the evaluations less informative about workers' talents.
- Strong incentives for individual performance may undermine team effort and team performance.
- Strong incentives for individual performance may mute effects of nonmonetary factors.

Although it is difficult to eliminate all of the unintended outcomes of the compensation system, the system should be designed with these outcomes in mind. The purpose of the compensation system in a firm is to induce the desired behavior of workers to achieve an organization's objectives. The effectiveness of each alternative way to reward personnel depends on external as well as internal factors that may affect workers' behavior. Compensation systems should balance costs and benefits to achieve the organization's objectives in recruitment, retention, and skill acquisition. Therefore, the organization's system of rewards can be viewed as a tool to achieve desired personnel outcomes.

Most of the factors identified in this report are important determinants of the effectiveness of the military compensation system. The pay system structure, the distribution of service members between grades and occupations, the members' progression through the ranks, the nature of performance evaluations, and job characteristics can affect decisions to recruit, reenlist, acquire important skills, and be innovative. The economics literature provides a method for looking at these effects together as a coherent system and for outlining how these effects might constrain or facilitate military transformation goals. Furthermore, the peculiarities of the military compensation system may limit some of the unintended outcomes that can arise.

Although the economics literature provides many useful insights into how a compensation system operates, it has some notable weaknesses. First, with the exception of a few studies, available theoretical literature is not directly applicable to the peculiarities of the military compensation system. Second, a lack of empirical studies constrains understanding of whether the theoretical arguments are important determinants of workers' behavior. Third, few studies look at the systems of rewards as a coherent mechanism, where different methods of inducing performance and sorting interact. This report considers these limitations while examining what economic models suggest for the efforts of the military transformation.

ACKNOWLEDGMENTS

I would like to thank Beth Asch for insightful guidance and suggestions on earlier versions of this report, and James Hosek for his helpful comments and constructive reviews. This report also benefited from the discussions with LTC Jeffrey Peterson and Major Thomas Edison, fellows at the Pardee RAND Graduate School. The quality of the report was substantially improved by the comments of reviewers Nicole Maestas and Jim Dertouzos of RAND. Input from Jennifer Lee and Shelley Wiseman helped to improve structure and editing of the document. Finally, I would like to thank Jennifer Kavanagh for her help in reviewing the report. Any remaining mistakes are of the author.

1. INTRODUCTION

Evaluating the relationship between the goals of military transformation and the military compensation and personnel management systems is an important and timely topic. Efforts are under way to transform the U.S. military into more agile and easily deployable forces with capabilities to react to a range of contingencies. Transformation changes the way the military is organized and the way it is conducting its operations. It requires a shift to a new paradigm of defense planning and implementation. For example, a transformed Army will be built around smaller, lighter, faster, highly networked units that are quicker to get into a fight. But more important, transformation changes what is expected from the personnel. Men and women in uniform should be encouraged to think and act creatively, be proactive, and take well-calculated risks.[1]

The current military compensation and personnel management system, however, may not be able to fully satisfy these transformation goals. Although the current system was successful in adapting to the challenges of the external and internal environment in the past, there are several areas that might hinder the efforts of recent initiatives. It is suggested that the rewards system lacks flexibility. For example, it creates senior careers that may be too short, as service members are induced to separate after 20 years of service and are not allowed to serve past 30 years of service.[2] Moreover, an up-or-out promotion rule may induce good performers to leave the military too early if they perceive little chance of promotion.

But the most important concern is that the system supports status quo thinking rather than a culture of innovation. The current military compensation system encourages conformity in performance and creates incentives to play it safe and does not place any emphasis on flexibility, well-calculated risk-taking, and out-of-the-box thinking throughout the military organization (see Asch and Hosek, 2004).

---

[1] See DoD (2002b).

[2] See, for example, Garamone (2003a, 2003b).

Therefore, the military compensation and personnel system can benefit from changes that would allow for greater flexibility to manage personnel, create incentives for reasonable risk-taking and innovation, permit greater creativity in various phases of military activity, and support more decentralized forces.[3]

To add to the policy discussion, this report reviews economic models of compensation and incentives with the emphasis on flexibility and the goals of transformation. Previous studies found the economics compensation and incentives literature to be very useful for modeling the military compensation system (Asch, 1993). The theory of military compensation uses economic models of compensation to describe underlying behavior of personnel and to connect it to the objectives of the military. For example, Asch and Warner (1994b) develop a theory of military compensation and personnel policy. The model that they develop allows considering effects of different approaches to compensating personnel and various personnel management rules. This review extends the previous studies by exploring how different models of incentives can help create an incentives structure compatible with the goals of military transformation.

The goal of the economics compensation and incentives literature is to describe how the pay structure affects the types of people that are attracted to a firm, how hard they work, and what outcomes can be expected. These studies recognize that workers will perform better if they are rewarded for additional effort. Moreover, they suggest that the structure of compensation and performance measures determines the outcomes that persist in the organization. Models of compensation that this report discusses describe different forms that these rewards can take. Rank-order tournaments, career incentives, and pay-for-performance and nonmonetary rewards all try to ensure that the best people are selected into a firm and that they work hard. However, these models are different in how they ensure that good workers are selected and stay in the firm, in the type of reward for additional effort, possible unintended outcomes, and the implementation costs for each scheme. The

_____

[3] For a discussion of what transformation means for the military compensation and personnel policies, see Asch and Hosek (2004).

remainder of this report describes each of the models of compensation in more detail.

The following set of questions helps understand the models of compensation.

- o Why is a particular paradigm attractive for modeling the behavior of the personnel in the military?
- o What are the benefits to the organization? How does the paradigm ensure that the best people are selected and retained and that they exert optimal effort?
- o What are the paradigm's administrative costs?
- o What are some possible unintended outcomes, both good and bad? Judging from available evidence, under what conditions are these outcomes likely to occur in practice?
- o Can the paradigm be implemented in the military?
- o Does the paradigm support the objectives of military transformation?

It is also important to outline the limits to the scope of this report. First, this report covers a limited scope of models. For example, it does not review models that examine human capital development in the organization. It does not consider factors that affect job satisfaction, nor does it explore in detail the issues of implementing different policies.[4] It mainly covers how the current system of incentives may constrain or facilitate the goals of transformation. Moreover, it is limited in the extent of the analysis. This report provides a literature review of the relevant models; it identifies the factors that are important for the military compensation system. However, it is left to further analysis within this project to determine which of the alternatives may be best for aligning incentives in military compensation with the goals of transformation.

This report is organized around models of compensation and several extensions of existing theory on this topic.

- o Section 2 describes how incentives are provided through a system of promotions in the hierarchical organization. This model of compensation is directly applicable to the military compensation system where most increases in pay come through promotions and change of rank.
- o Section 3 provides an overview of the theory of work-life incentives and pensions.
- o Section 4 reviews how incentives are provided when rewards are directly linked to performance.

---

[4] For a good guide into implementing pay-for-performance policies, see Risher (2004).

o Section 5 describes how teamwork is rewarded in the military.
o Section 6 outlines how nonmonetary factors can affect performance in hierarchical organizations.
o Finally, Section 7 draws conclusions and connects the economics literature to the efforts of military transformation.

2. PROMOTION TOURNAMENTS

The first model of compensation that this report discusses is a rank-order tournament system. Among all the models of compensation discussed in this report, the tournament system is the most applicable to the military compensation and personnel management system. Its application follows from the hierarchical structure of the ranks in the military. This section reviews the theory of the rank-order tournament system, outlines how it relates to the military compensation system, and evaluates whether this paradigm supports the objectives of the military transformation. Note that the models presented in this section are also related to the models of career incentives discussed in Section 3.

THE TOURNAMENT SYSTEM

What Is the Promotion Tournament System?

Compensation in a hierarchical organization ties the performance of workers to the organization's structure and to their promotion through the ranks or grades. Researchers who have analyzed the personnel files of a large firm found that most pay increases come from changes in jobs or job titles and that there is little variation in pay within job grades (Gibbs and Hendricks, 1995). This finding justifies economists' interest in how promotions from one grade to another create incentives for performance.

Lazear and Rosen (1981) were the first to suggest looking at the incentive effects of promotion schemes through the prism of rank-order tournament theory, following the analogy of sports competitions in which a fixed number of contestants compete for a fixed number of predetermined rewards. The rewards are set in advance, and the agents exert effort to increase the likelihood of winning a better prize or of being promoted. During the selection process, candidates are compared either to some predetermined standard or to other candidates. Based on past performance, the selection committee determines who has sufficient skills, experience, and leadership potential to fit the available position at the higher levels of organization.

Promotions Are the Key Feature of Managing Personnel in the Military

Asch and Warner (1994b) were the first to view military compensation from the perspective of tournament theory. As in other hierarchical organizations considered by Lazear and Rosen (1981), military service members progress through the ranks by getting promoted. In other words, compensation is mostly determined by a rank-order tournament, in the sense that the compensation structure is predetermined and the promotion criteria are defined. Military rank determines basic pay and basic allowances for housing. The largest share of regular military compensation is basic pay.[5] The services share the same basic pay table for officers, enlisted personnel, and warrant officers. The basic pay table includes an amount for each pay grade[6] as well as incremental longevity steps to reflect the length of service. Together, the pay levels in each grade and the longevity steps determine the structure of the basic pay table, while increases in pay due to promotion are relatively more important.

THE TOURNAMENT SYSTEM'S ATTRACTION

The literature on rank-order tournaments highlights several reasons why this approach to modeling system of rewards is attractive. All of these points are relevant to the military compensation system. First, promotions provide strong incentives. Employees who want to be promoted try to work hard to outperform their colleagues. This creates incentives even without immediate monetary reward. Second, regular evaluations can help sort workers into jobs based on their abilities. Over time, those employees who fit the description of the job on the next level tend to be promoted. Below, the report elaborates on these points described in the economics and incentives literature.

---

[5] See Asch, Hosek, and Martin (2002) for a detailed description of different parts of cash compensation in the military.

[6] Pay grades are connected to the military ranks: E-1 through E-9 for enlisted personnel, O-1 through O-10 for officers, and W-1 through W-5 for warrant officers.

The Possibility of Promotion Induces Employees to Outperform Their Colleagues

Unlike explicit pay-for-performance compensation methods, which are discussed in this report in Section 4, pay in the tournament system does not directly recognize performance. The pay table is set in advance, and pay does not reflect immediate performance or output. The promotion process provides incentives by choosing the best worker from those eligible for promotion from the next lower grade. The possibility of being promoted and earning a higher salary induces employees to outperform their colleagues and assume tasks that are more challenging. This creates incentives for performance as strong as explicit pay-for-performance mechanisms (see Section 4 of this report).

Effects of the tournament system on individual performance depend on the individual's expectation of rewards from promotion. Two factors determine this effect: the probability of promotion and the pay increase associated with promotion. All else equal, an increase in pay induces a worker to work harder. The increase in pay due to promotion affects how much effort workers exert. If the between-rank pay spread increases, workers have more incentive to perform better.[7]

The other factor that affects the strength of incentives is the probability of promotion, which depends on the number of people who compete for promotions, their relative quality, and the number of vacancies available. An increase in the probability of promotion induces a worker to exert more effort up to the point at which the probability is high enough so that additional effort has little effect. At one extreme, when the probability of promotion is 100 percent and the worker is certain of the outcome, there is no incentive to work harder. At the other extreme, when the probability is near zero, the worker also has little incentive to exert more effort in response to an increase in the probability. Therefore, the incentive effect is largest when the probability is near one-half or when the odds of getting promoted are even.

---

[7] Tests of the predictions of the tournament theory using results from golf tournaments support this claim (see Ehrenberg and Bognanno, 1990a, 1990b).

When the structure of pay between ranks is fixed, an organization can improve incentives for good performance by promoting better workers faster. When the pay level is the same for everyone, better workers are relatively worse off, they lack incentives to perform better, and they might be more likely to leave the organization if their skills are recognized in other organizations. By promoting its better workers faster, an organization induces hard work and retention. The evidence from the military compensation system supports these predictions of the tournament theory. Holding years of service constant, personnel with higher Armed Forces Qualification Test (AFQT) scores tend to occupy higher grades (Asch and Warner, 1994b, p. 109). Although all personnel in the same rank receive the same basic pay, the differences in compensation arise from the difference in promotion patterns; some workers are promoted more quickly than others. Asch, Hosek, and Martin (2002) estimate that variations in the regular military compensation of enlisted personnel increase over an individual's career, reflecting increasing differences in the speed of promotions.

The Tournament System Helps Sort Workers into Jobs

In addition to providing an incentive effect, the tournament system provides a way of learning about workers' abilities and promoting the workers based on their talents (see Green and Stokey, 1983). When a newcomer starts working in the organization, little is known about his quality or skills. Over time, however, the worker's quality is revealed, as his or her performance is compared to that of his or her peers or to some predetermined standard. During these evaluations, a worker gains a reputation and the organization learns about the worker's skills. In this way, the promotion system identifies better workers and helps assign better people to the higher grades of the organization where their skills are used in the best way. This factor is practically important to the military, because it wants to ensure that enough high-quality workers are available at all grades of the hierarchy because they provide a pool of capabilities at each grade and also contribute to the pool of candidates to fill in positions in the higher ranks.[8] Distribution of rewards between grades determines whether the most able workers are elevated to the top of the hierarchy. Rosen (1982) suggests that compensation skewed to favor higher-level employees helps attract workers at the bottom of the organization because high-productivity workers expect to be promoted to higher grades.

Available evidence supports the hypothesis that military promotions help to identify better service members. Following Ward and Tan (1985), Hosek and Mattock (2003) use AFQT and speed of promotion to E-4 and E-5 to infer the quality of enlisted personnel, given their occupational specialty and year of entry. Using this broader definition of quality that incorporates performance while in the military, they find that higher-quality personnel are more likely to stay in the military after the first term. In contrast, when quality is measured only by AFQT, the measure available at entry, there is practically no relationship between retention and quality. These findings suggest that the military compensation and promotion systems create incentives for high-quality workers to stay and perform in the organization.

THE TOURNAMENT SYSTEM'S ADMINISTRATIVE COSTS

Administrative requirements of the system are very important for learning how the compensation system may support or constrain the goals of the military transformation. Two factors are important in the tournament system. First, any compensation system requires a method of

---

[8] High-quality personnel are quite important to the military. Available evidence suggests that high-quality personnel are more likely to complete their initial term, so they are a better training investment than lesser-quality personnel. Furthermore, AFQT is strongly related to the education ultimately attained: the average AFQT score of high-school graduates is about 50, of people with some college by age 30 about 65, and of college graduates about 84 (Asch, Hosek, and Warner, 2001). Higher-scoring personnel pay off in terms of higher performance, yielding greater military capability. For example, higher-aptitude personnel performed better in operating Patriot missiles (Orvis, Childress, and Polich, 1992). In addition, positive effects of higher AFQT scores have also been found for tank crews (Scribner et al., 1986), multichannel radio communications (Winkler, Fernandez, and Polich, 1992), and ship readiness (Junor and Oi, 1996). See Kavanagh (2005) for the review of derminants of productivity for military personnel.

evaluating workers. In the tournament model, the evaluation system should provide some information about the person's performance relative to other workers to identify those people who are better than their colleagues and should be promoted. Second, the promotion system requires a flow of people through the hierarchy. The probability of promotion to the next round depends on whether there are vacancies in the higher grade. Lack of vacancies creates negative performance incentives for workers who expect that the reward for higher effort is more distant. Next these issues are discussed in more detail and provide examples of how the military compensation system is designed to take them into account.

The Tournament Model Requires a System of Evaluating Workers

Periodic evaluations of workers play an important role in the system of incentives. On the one hand, evaluations provide information to the firm about high-performing workers. On the other hand, evaluations provide feedback to the worker about his or her performance, as well as about what is expected from him or her. This report concentrates on the first factor due to its paramount importance to the system of incentives.

In the perfect world, the firm would like to reward each worker depending on his or her performance. People can be rewarded on inputs or outputs, as well as according to the social benefits that they provide. However, the costs of measuring performance can be a significant part of the system's administrative requirements. Any measure of performance will reflect a combination of factors. It will include the real effect of the worker (how hard the worker performed, how much effort he or she exerted); the effect of the difficulty of the job and factors that affect operational goals; and effect of chance (Klerman, 2005). Often it is very costly to distinguish between different parts.

The tournament system has the ability to decrease some of the costs of measuring performance. Promotions based on relative performance evaluations might be more cost efficient than measuring absolute performance levels (Mookherjee, 1984). This approach reduces the effect of random factors that are common to all individuals (Green and Stokey,

1983). For example, all military recruiters will be similarly affected by an increase in interest in joining the military, and so their relative outcomes should be unaffected by this. When measuring the absolute level of performance is costly, relative performance evaluations (or grading on a curve) provide a considerable advantage.

Note, however, that relative evaluations do not work well when employees are facing quite different working conditions or are working on projects that cannot be easily compared. In the military, geographical and occupational variation in tasks may render relative performance evaluation less efficient. One should not directly compare workers in different regions of the country, if the regional effects on performance are very large. Differences between job conditions may make this approach to determining performance less reliable.

The Promotion Tournament System Relies on People Flowing Throughout the Hierarchy

The tournament system requires a mechanism that facilitates learning about promotion opportunities. The effects of the promotion system are strong only if workers are able to evaluate their probability of promotion. A lack of vacancies at higher grades decreases the probability of promotions and the likelihood that workers will exert more than the usual level of effort. Thus, an organization must ensure that enough positions are vacated in each grade of the organization each particular year. In private-sector organizations, vacancies are created by promotions and through expansion of the business, otherwise organizations may have to create rules that help separate people and create vacancies to manage the flow of workers through the hierarchy. These rules, however, are costly, as they might create outflow of workers from the organization.

The military services have distinct rules that govern the flow of people through the hierarchy. Promotion in the military follows up-or-out rules that are rare in large private firms (Baker, Jensen, and Murphy, 1988). These rules require an individual to be promoted to the next highest grade within a specified period of time in order to remain in the service. For example, enlisted personnel should be promoted to grade E-5 within eight years of service, and to E-6 within 21 years of service. Those who are not promoted within this period face mandatory separation (Asch and Warner, 1994b). On one hand, these rules facilitate the flow of individuals through the hierarchy by providing vacancies for promotions of workers from the lower ranks (Asch and Warner, 1994b, 2001b). The up-or-out rules are effective if they force out the least desirable personnel.[9] On the other hand, these rules are costly in terms of the loss of personnel who could continue to be valuable in their current positions. For example, workers in technical occupations might not value the leadership positions associated with promotion, although they are very productive in their current jobs.

As an alternative to creating special rules that manage the flow of personnel throughout the career, an organization can change the structure of payoffs between grades. To maintain incentives for performance across the hierarchy, a lower probability of promotion should be accompanied by an increase in the rewards that a particular person gets. This report will discuss this alternative in more detail in Section 4.

THE TOURNAMENT SYSTEM'S UNINTENDED OUTCOMES

Unintended outcomes can arise in the tournament system. To derive lessons for the efforts of transformation, it is important to understand how the unintended effects develop and under what conditions they are likely to occur in practice. First, the structure of compensation affects workers' risk-taking behavior. Workers are more likely to make more risky decisions if they believe that doing so can bring them the rewards of promotions. Second, the evaluation system might create incentives for workers and managers to play the system. Workers might redirect their efforts to unproductive activities with an aim to divert the promotion decision in their favor. Third, the promotion system has the potential to undermine teamwork and cooperation. If workers are rewarded solely on their individual performance, they might be less inclined to help their teammates. Finally, the literature suggests that performance might decline after promotion if the evaluation system

---

[9] The usual explanation for the up-or-out rules in the private sector is that they weed out the unproductive (Kahn and Huberman, 1988).

cannot effectively identify what factors are important for performance on the next level.

The Compensation Structure Affects a Worker's Behavior and Willingness to Take Risks

In the tournament system, attitude toward risk and high effort depends on subjectively evaluated probability of promotion. The best performers are not inclined to work hard and take excessive risks because they are pretty sure in their win (Baker, Jensen, and Murphy, 1988). In the military, one can expect that the best performers would rather play it safe and not jeopardize the likelihood of promotion. They need only to exert enough effort to outdo their rivals or to achieve the performance standard, even though they may be capable of even higher productivity levels.

In the tournament system, one can expect increased risk-taking from the workers who are on the margin between promotion and no promotion. For these workers, additional effort can significantly change their rewards in the near future. Therefore, one can expect them to work harder and undertake more risks.[10] Available evidence from the business environment supports this proposition. Knoeber and Thurman (1994) tested tournament theory on agricultural producers, who are rewarded not only by the quantity they produce but also by their performance relative to other growers. The authors observed that more-capable agents chose less-risky strategies, while less-capable growers varied greatly. Brown, Harlow, and Starks (1996) present similar evidence regarding investment portfolio managers, who were evaluated relative to their colleagues. Those portfolio managers who had a bad midyear evaluation were more likely to invest in more risky assets to increase the probability of gaining a better performance evaluation at the end of the year.

---

[10] Available evidence from athletic tournaments supports this point. Ehrenberg and Bognanno (1990a, 1990b) suggest that performance early in the golf tournament did not appear to be correlated with financial rewards. However, the contestants' behavior changed in the last round, when information about the prospects of winning was readily available. The golfers who had better scores before the last round and still could influence the outcome of the tournament improved their performance more than other golfers. Similar evidence is documented in studies of auto racing (Becker and Huselid, 1992).

The trade-off between risk-taking and compensation is very important in the military compensation system. The military would like soldiers and officers who are not afraid to take calculated risks. However, as mentioned by Collins and Jacobs (2002), the military has developed a culture of zero tolerance for mistakes. Given intense competition for limited command and promotion opportunities, officers cannot afford to fail. An innovative decision that has a slight chance of failing will not be considered because it can slow down the service member's promotion path. This may inhibit risk-taking. In fact, it may overinhibit risk-taking relative to the level desired in a transformed military. Within a simple framework, the workers would decide how much risk to undertake by comparing the increased chance of promotion if the risk pays off to the decreased chance of promotion if the risk fails. However, a change to what is considered a good promotion could shift this behavior.

Subjective Evaluations May Inspire Unproductive Behavior by Workers and Managers

Subjective evaluations are widely used in the military compensation system as well as in the private sector.[11] In the military, in addition to objective measures of performance, such as physical performance tests, tests of abilities, numbers of courses taken, and weapons qualifications, promotions are based on subjective evaluations by supervisors about potential in the next position, ability to handle stress, and tactical exercise outcomes. This information is used to determine whether the worker has the skills and experience necessary for a higher position. These subjective measures mitigate distortions created by imperfect objective measures[12] and that a combination of

---

[11] For studies of subjective evaluations in the private sector, see Baker, Gibbons, and Murphy (1994), Gibbs et al. (2002), and Ittner, Larcker, and Meyer (2003).

[12] Using data from the sales and services departments in automobile dealerships, Gibbs et al. (2002) show that subjective evaluations are used to improve awards that are based only on the quantitative performance measures. For example, subjective evaluations were more likely if the bonus were calculated on some difficult-to-achieve formula. In this case, subjective evaluations are designed to provide

objective and subjective evaluations may be optimal (Baker, Gibbons, and Murphy, 1994). These evaluations, however, have several shortcomings.

In recent years, the economics literature started to recognize some unintended outcomes associated with subjective evaluations. One outcome is that workers may spend time trying to influence managers' decisions (Milgrom, 1988). For example, a worker who wants to influence the assignment of bonuses might be extremely attentive to the manager making the decisions, or the worker might try to provide the manager with information about who should receive a bonus.

Milgrom (1988) suggests that these influence activities provide both a benefit and a cost. Influence activities can provide the manager with valuable information. However, the activities require time and effort that could otherwise have been spent on more productive activities or enjoyed as leisure. Milgrom (1988) also suggests that the prevalence of influence activities is usually connected to the amount of power a manager has. Workers are more likely to want to influence managers who have a good deal of discretion about matters that affect workers' welfare. Thus, managers whose decisions most strongly affect workers' welfare are more likely to face solicitations from workers. To limit influence activities, Milgrom (1988) suggests limiting the discretion of managers, especially for matters that have consequences for many workers in an organization. Alternatively, influence activities can be limited if managers' decisions are not susceptible to the information received from workers. At the cost of additional effort, managers can increase the reliability of subjective measures. They can diversify the sources of information about workers or improve monitoring of the workers' efforts. For example, many private companies use 360-degree evaluations that gather information about a specific person's performance from his or her supervisors, peers, subordinates, and even clients.

---

incentives for performance in cases where achieving the final output as measured by objective measures is difficult to accomplish.

There is the possibility that influence activities can arise in the military.[13] When meetings with supervisors are infrequent, personnel may exert extra effort when they can impress their managers and may under-perform when interaction with supervisors is not likely. This, however, is only a hypothesis. The evidence about effectiveness of subjective evaluations in the military is limited, and a number of rival hypotheses can be used to explore these issues.

Subjective evaluations can also be associated with favoritism (Prendergast and Topel, 1996). If managers care about how their decisions affect workers, they are likely to favor some employees over others.[14] For example, a manager might give a bonus to an employee not on merit, but because of personal preferences. Prendergast and Topel (1996) suggest several ways to limit favoritism in organizations. One approach is to limit rewards associated with promotions. In this case, managers will know that their decisions will not significantly affect workers' welfare and might be less likely to favor one or another candidate. Another solution is to limit the role an individual manager plays in the promotion decision. For example, in the military services, promotion boards are used in determining who will be promoted to the higher rank, and evaluations from several people might be used.

A Promotion System Can Undermine Teamwork and Cooperation

Another important issue with the tournament system and its relationship to the military is that the incentives created by a

---

[13] Results from the survey of the Air Force officers conducted by Wayland (2002) suggest that several factors are more important in the current evaluation system than is actual performance. Those include supervisor's writing skills, subjectivity, inflation of the rewards, halo effect, and sponsorship. Although the extent of the problem cannot be judged from these results, it provides some evidence that the problems exist.

[14] An important part of the model that Prendergast and Topel (1996) developed is that supervisors value the power to affect the lives of their subordinates. This can be true if one considers that firms are social institutions where personal relations between workers are important components of the daily routine. This may create divergence between the objectives of managers and the objectives of the firm. However, this effect can be muted if managers are judged on their performance in making evaluations.

tournament system can undermine team effort and cooperation between service members. Lazear (1989) suggests that a large gap between winners and losers in the tournament produces a substitution effect between helping and individual effort. If incentives for individual performance increase, workers are less likely to help each other or to cooperate, because it can hurt their relative performance. If two workers are competing for a single promotion, cooperation between them is likely to be minimal, because one worker's success implies the other's failure. However, in most instances in the military, promotion competition is not for a single position. It is, therefore, unlikely that service members have an incentive not to cooperate with peers who are also seeking promotion. Furthermore, subjective evaluations probably take into account how well a person has cooperated with other team members. This suggests that it is probably advantageous for the teammates to cooperate.

In addition to reducing cooperation, workers can also undertake nonproductive activities to make their rivals look worse. Workers in the organization can pursue two types of activities—they can work on their own project, or they can take actions that decrease performance of other members of the organization. When the promotion system rewards relative performance, workers have an incentive to devote effort to making their counterparts look worse, because it increases their own chances of promotion. These activities are often referred to as sabotage (Chen, 2003; Auriol, Friebel, and Pechlivanos, 2002). Chen (2003) suggests that the probability of sabotage activities increases when the number of candidates increases and there are several leaders who are easy to identify. In this case, nonleaders have strong incentives to increase sabotage activities against those with greater ability. Furthermore, the likelihood of sabotage is higher when the reward for the promotion is large, because workers have larger incentives to succeed. However, several factors limit applications of these studies to the military. For example, in the military, sabotage might not prevail because teammates might not be competing for the same promotions. Furthermore, sabotage might be easy to identify, and the whole team might suffer because of it.

THE TOURNAMENT SYSTEM'S RELEVANCE TO MILITARY TRANSFORMATION

This section has described the model of the promotion tournament and provided examples of how military compensation can be modeled using the tournament system. It examined the system's benefits, reviewed possible administrative requirements, and considered possible unintended outcomes. The remainder of this section examines how the tournament is relevant for the efforts of military transformation. First, it briefly mentions how the military compensation system fits into the paradigm of the tournament system. Then it summarizes the main factors that may be important for the efforts of the military transformation. Finally, it suggests how the paradigm can support the goals of the transformed military.

The Tournament System Fits the Military Compensation System

As described throughout this section, the tournament system fits well the realities of the military compensation system. Most of the increase in pay for service members comes through change in rank. Competition for promotions ensures that service members exert enough effort in those performance areas that are measured and that matter for positive evaluation necessary for promotion.

Many Elements of the Tournament System Are Important in the Military

There are several elements that determine individual performance under the tournament system. Service members are making decisions about how hard to work based on their subjective evaluations of the rewards from promotion. At least two factors affect these evaluations: pay in the next grade and probability of promotion. Although the pay in the rank is fixed through the pay table, this does not mean that service members can accurately predict their probability of promotion. Uncertainty of available vacancies, influence activities, and favoritism can distort evaluations of promotion probabilities and consequently distort the incentives that the tournament system provides.

There are important patterns of effects that the tournament system has on attitudes toward high effort and risk-taking. As described previously, the tournament system does not provide incentives for outstanding performance. Highly qualified workers need only to work hard enough to outperform their rivals, even though they may be capable of even higher productivity levels. They would rather play it safe, afraid to jeopardize their promotions. Only marginal workers have incentives to exert extraordinary efforts and take calculated risks in order to increase their probability of promotion.

Furthermore, those incentives are only to produce in the fields that are rewarded. Measures of performance play an important role in shaping the behavior of workers. These measures can be objective, or number-driven, as well as subjective.

Organizations have several ways to change performance outcomes. They can change the structure of compensation between grades, they can decide to reward different activities by changing metrics of performance, or they can change the performance evaluation system. Furthermore, organizations should regularly provide enough vacancies to promote good performers and separate underperformers.

How Can the Paradigm Support the Objectives of Military Transformation?

There are two main concerns about the current military compensation system. First, the system may not provide enough flexibility to support decentralized forces, to allow reaction to possible contingencies, and to provide sufficient variation in military careers. For example, researchers suggest that military compensation produces retention outcomes that are similar between different occupations (Asch and Hosek, 2004). Another concern is that the system does not support the culture of innovation and encourages conformity in performance.

There is no easy way to change the system so that it can support the goals of military transformation. Most of the elements of the current military compensation system are playing an important role in shaping performance and influencing behavior of workers. For example, to allow more flexibility in managing careers, the military might introduce a system that allows rewarding service members without promoting them, allows more flexibility in selecting careers, and allows for more flexibility in selecting assignments. But these changes can intervene with the current rules that are in effect. For example, this can include changing the nature of the one-size-fits-all system and allowing different career progressions. But military personnel have much confidence in the system that is the same for everyone.

There are already examples of flexible use of the current system in the military. For instance, a special system of managing warrant officers allows keeping in the services personnel whose assignments are repetitive in nature and do not offer broadening experiences required as preparation for higher command (see Fernandez, 2002). There are only three restrictions on managing warrant officers:[15] legislation limits the number of warrant officers in the top W-5 rank, establishes uniform procedures for the operation of warrant officer promotion boards, and requires separation of warrant officers who were twice passed over for promotion to the next grade. Despite those restrictions, the legislation provides considerable flexibility in managing warrant officers, and the services use their warrant officer systems in remarkably different ways.[16] Another example of the flexibilities available in the current system is the career tracks in the Army that officers can pursue after promotion to the rank of major. Although the officers are still subject to the same pay table, they are managed, professionally developed, assigned, and promoted according to their branch or functional area's requirements.

Moreover, some changes are warranted to induce more innovation and risk-taking activities. Even the current system can support these objectives, provided that the innovative activities and well-calculated risk-taking is recognized in the performance evaluation process. Most of the effort should be directed toward determining how these activities can be measured and rewarded. But it will be very difficult to develop precise metrics to evaluate these activities.

In the end, the decision about what factors to change and what changes to make should compare the costs and benefits of different suggestions. To make the system more flexible, it is possible to sacrifice some elements, while not ruining the system overall. Cost

---

[15] Warrant officers are managed according to the Warrant Officer Management Act, which was passed as part of the National Defense Authorization Act for Fiscal Years 1992 and 1993.

[16] See Fernandez (2002) for an overview.

effectiveness of different alternatives should be the main comparison factor.

Although the tournament system by itself can provide more flexibility than it currently does, the effects can be evaluated better when considering predictions of other systems of compensation. The next several sections review these models of compensation. For example, some elements of the compensation system can be more fully explained using career incentive schemes, while the effectiveness of the measures of performance can be better explained by pay-for-performance mechanisms.

3. CAREER INCENTIVE SCHEMES: DEFERRED COMPENSATION AND RETIREMENT PAY

In the military, examples are easily found of rewards for good performance being deferred. Pay associated with promotion is one example. Another example is retirement pay. A set of economic models that describes incentives created by deferred pay is called a career incentive scheme. This section reviews these models, evaluates how they relate to military compensation, and outlines how they relate to military transformation objectives. Implications from these models should be examined together with the implications from other models, such as promotion tournaments (see Section 2).

EXAMPLES OF CAREER INCENTIVES

A set of economic models describes how compensation can be connected to the career path that employees follow over time. These models are called career incentive schemes. Examples from the public and private sectors suggest that when workers stay in an organization for a long time, employers can pay them less in some periods and more in others.[17] For example, deferred compensation, whereby workers are paid less in early years and more late in their careers, follows this model. Deferred payments of this type serve as career incentives, where current performance is rewarded through future pay increases.

Promotion Ladders as Deferred Compensation

This report emphasizes two examples of deferred compensation that are relevant to the military compensation system. The first form of deferred compensation that arises within hierarchical job structures is the promotion ladder. A worker's performance in the current period is

---

[17] Empirical studies describe several examples of deferred compensation in the private sector. Medoff and Abraham (1981) report that among workers performing tasks of comparable difficulty, those with greater experience receive higher pay, even when their performance is not superior. They found that among managers and professionals staying in a job over an extended period of time, relative earnings rose, but relative performance either remained constant or fell over time. Similar evidence is provided by Kotlikoff and Gokhale (1992) and Lazear and Moore (1984).

rewarded through higher pay in the future, when promotions to higher positions provide increased compensation. This model, however, is different from the tournament system discussed in Section 2, because it does not require that some people not be promoted. In a deferred compensation scheme, it is possible to have a promotion ladder where everyone is promoted; the distinguishing feature is that pay is structured to increase with longevity whether or not productivity increases. To the extent that promotion brings jumps in pay but part of the increase in pay is deferred, tournament and deferred compensation schemes intersect.

Retirement Pay as Deferred Compensation

Another form of deferred compensation is retirement pay. Two main paradigms of retirement pay are possible. Pensions can be determined through specific formulas or through individual contributions. Friedberg and Webb (2003) note that defined benefit plans[18] have become considerably less common in the United States since the early 1980s, while defined contribution plans[19] have spread. Moreover, pensions differ with respect to when the plan is vested, years of service required, inflation protection, and levels of benefits. Defined benefit and defined contribution plans are both deferred compensation schemes in that the worker cannot receive the benefit until reaching retirement eligibility. However, under some plans it is possible to borrow against the accumulated retirement wealth for certain purposes, e.g., to finance college expenses.

Retirement pay is a central feature of the current personnel system. Current military retirement pay is vested at 20 years of service when service members are eligible to collect the benefits. This is

---

[18] A defined benefit plan usually determines retirement benefits as a function of earnings, tenure, and retirement age. The retirement wealth under this plan usually accumulates slowly early in the job, accelerates after a predetermined period of tenure, and declines after a certain age.

[19] In a defined contribution plan, the retirement fund is simply a sum of contributions that the worker and/or employers made throughout a career plus the growth or contraction of the fund over time as an investment vehicle, so that, from the worker's perspective, the timing of pension wealth accrual is not tied to the timing of retirement.

different from the experience of the private sector where the pension is required to be fully vested after five or seven years of work.[20] Workers who leave the military before completing 20 years of service receive no retirement benefit.[21] However, the chance of receiving retirement pay can create important incentives for performance and sorting for midcareer personnel. There are several advantages as well as disadvantages associated with the retirement system in the military.[22]

WHY DEFERRING COMPENSATION INTO THE FUTURE IS ATTRACTIVE

Economics literature suggests several reasons that deferring compensation into the future is attractive. First, deferring rewards into the future may help select better workers into jobs. If pay is deferred, the firm attracts workers who are more likely to stay longer in the firm. Second, delayed rewards can induce better performance. Young workers would like to gain their reputation and work hard in the start of their career. Third, retirement pay ensures that workers perform well in the organization until they separate. This report elaborates on these points next.

Deferred Compensation Induces Selection of Workers

Salop and Salop (1976) suggest that deferring compensation improves selection of workers. When an individual joins a firm, the organization spends time and resources training the new employee. These investments are lost if the worker decides to leave the firm. Therefore, an

---

[20] The vesting provisions are determined by the Employee Retirement Income Security Act (United States Code, Title 29). A firm can choose between two vesting schedules. It can either fully vest the pension after the person worked for the firm for five years, or gradually give the worker right to a percentage of his or her accrued benefit derived from the employer contribution so that the pension is partially vested after three years and fully vested after seven years of service.

[21] As reported in the *Ninth Quadrennial Review of Military Compensation*, only about 18 percent of the cohort of new service members are expected to qualify for retirement benefits (DoD, 2002a). In particular, about 46 percent of new officers and about 16 percent of new enlisted personnel would start in the military long enough to receive retirement pay (DoD, 2002a).

[22] For a detailed overview of the advantages and disadvantages of the military retirement system, see Asch and Warner (1994a, 1994b) and Asch, Johnson, and Warner (1998).

organization would like to ensure that the worker either pays for the training or stays with the firm long enough to repay the investments through increased productivity. By deferring compensation, the firm attracts workers who are more likely to stay with the firm. Ideally, the worker's propensity to stay with the firm will not be negatively correlated with productivity. One can expect that productive workers are more likely to stay in the organization longer, because over time, a worker's ability can be revealed. This effect should be very strong in the military compensation system, because retirement is vested at 20 years of service. When vesting of retirement pay is delayed, only those who think that they can achieve the required rank and longevity will decide to pursue a career in the military, while others will leave.

Delayed Rewards Can Encourage Better Performance

Another reason for deferring rewards into the future may be that deferred compensation provides incentives for performance (Lazear, 1981). If wages grow with experience and inherent productivity does not, older workers will receive wages that are higher than their productivity would indicate while younger workers receive wages that are less than their productivity would deem appropriate. If the premiums given to older workers are large enough, they will work harder to retain their jobs than they would in the absence of the premium.

Deferred compensation schemes also provide incentives for young workers because they want to invest in their reputation. A good reputation can lead either to the higher wage growth within a firm or to better future offers in the market (Fama, 1980). In the military, nothing is quite as visible as promotion, and, among the higher ranks, promotion opportunities and assignments after promotion depend highly upon one's reputation. This induces personnel to spend energy and time on those tasks that build reputation, whether or not they are good for their unit's performance. It suggests that reputation effect in the military may persist throughout the career. Hosek and Mattock (2003) show that enlisted personnel who are promoted faster to E-4 are also promoted faster to E-5, holding everything else constant. Reputation may play a role in promotions in both cases. Alternatively, the results may reflect the combined, persistent effect of a member's taste for military service, ability, and level of effort.

There are four conditions for career concerns in an organization to be an effective tool of motivating high performance (Holmstrom, 1982). First, performance on any given task should be visible to those who decide promotions. Second, current performance should provide information about productivity in future tasks. Third, workers should care about the future (i.e., they should not discount future outcomes too much). Fourth, information about individual performance should be available at low costs in external and internal markets.

Retirement Pay Strengthens Incentives for Performance

Lazear (1985) posits that retirement pay ensures that an employee continue to have an incentive to exert effort until the last day at work. Consider a worker without a pension who is working his or her last day on the job. The individual has a choice of exerting high effort or low effort. The threat of dismissal does not impede incentives to shirk, because the individual does not plan to work further anyway. Therefore, a simple compensation scheme might not be able to force people to provide enough effort in the last period. This problem can be avoided if an organization offers retirement pay that is conditional on the worker's effort in the final employment period. A worker who is caught shirking is fired and foregoes his pension. A large enough pension will serve as a mechanism to ensure satisfactory performance.[23]

The effectiveness of the incentives provided by the pension system depends to some degree on when the pension is vested. Lazear (1985) suggested that full and immediate vesting of the pension is always

---

[23] Lazear (1985) showed that a defined contribution plan provides optimal resource allocation. A defined benefits plan where pension depends only on the years of service and not on salary also provides optimal resource allocation. However, a defined benefits plan where the pension depends on the average salary and number of years worked induces too much work, too much effort, and too much human capital investment relative to the efficient use of resources. The problems with these plans arise when there is a difference between a worker's discount rate and an interest rate, when the worker does not know how the pension is determined, and when the employer does not know about the human capital that worker possesses and how it affects the worker's productivity.

efficient for the pension outcome; it guarantees that the worker's rewards over time are fully based on his or her productivity, whereas partial vesting would diminish the payoff to his or her productivity. Furthermore, even a no-vesting policy can be efficient when all workers leave either before or after a pension is vested.[24] However, vesting can create inefficiencies when there is enough variation in the workers' separation patterns.[25] If workers are significantly heterogeneous, different retirement schemes might be optimal and workers would self-select according to their preferences.

CAREER INCENTIVE SCHEMES' ADMINISTRATIVE COSTS

Several factors affect costs of administering career incentive schemes. First, the system of rewards should be skewed enough to attract better workers to stay in the organization for longer. This, however, can be quite an expensive approach because a worker may discount his or her future at a high rate. Furthermore, as explained below, career incentives suggest that personnel at career end earn wages that are higher than their performance would warrant. This requires a mechanism of separating workers at the pinnacle of their careers, when workers are overpaid relative to their productivity. The report elaborates on these factors next.

Career Incentive Schemes Require a Skewed Pay Structure

To encourage workers to exert more effort, the pay structure should be skewed. In other words, the salary increases associated with

---

[24] If all workers leave an organization before their pensions are vested, an efficient outcome is achieved through the scheme that rewards workers with their productivity in each period. If all workers tend to stay in the organization until after the pension is vested, an efficient effort level can also be achieved, because workers obtain their pension rewards.

[25] Lazear (1985) showed that, in this case, those workers who leave an organization before a pension is vested are relatively underpaid compared to those who stay. When a worker joins an organization, it is difficult to determine whether the worker will stay until the pension is vested or will leave. Therefore, an organization will deduct prospective retirement payments from wages. However, those workers who leave an organization before the pension is vested do not collect their benefits; thus they are underpaid compared to their contribution to the production process.

promotions at higher levels must be greater than those for lower levels. Empirical evidence from the private sector finds support for these claims.[26] The literature gives three reasons for this structure (Asch and Warner, 1994b). First, pay should be skewed to account for a decrease in the number of promotions available for workers in the higher grades. As employees are promoted through the hierarchy, they have fewer remaining promotions left in their career, so their incentives to work hard decline. Therefore, to sustain the level of effort, the reward associated with each successive promotion must go up. Second, pay should be skewed to represent the decline in the number of available vacancies. For workers in the lower levels of an organization, there may be many promotion opportunities available, but at the top of the organization, there are considerably fewer. Third, an increase in pay should account for an increase in responsibility for higher-ranked jobs. Rosen (1982) shows that returns on ability in hierarchical organizations are convex because better workers make better decisions at the top of the organization; thus, high-ability workers are more important in higher-ranked positions. As a result, the pay gain associated with a promotion must increase to induce the most talented workers to stay in the organization and seek advancement to the senior ranks where their ability is most valued.

The estimates from the simulation model of the Army enlisted force suggests that effects on performance of the skewed pay raises are bigger than for an across-the-board increase (Asch and Warner, 1994b; Asch, Johnson, and Warner 1998). Although the costs of the two alternatives are the same, giving an incrementally higher percentage pay increase to higher grades increases performance of the personnel substantially more.[27] In 2000, Congress began targeting military pay raises to mid-

---

[26] In a study of the compensation system in one firm, Baker, Gibbs, and Holmstrom (1994a) found that pay increases steeply with rank. For example, Level Six managers in the firm they studied earned about five times the amount earned by Level One managers. Main, O'Reilly, and Wade (1993), Abowd (1990), and Leonard (1990) report even larger differences at the top level of large firms, where the CEO typically earns four to five times as much as managers three levels below.

[27] The index of performance increased from 100 to 153 for the entire force and from 135 to 210 for E-7s (Asch and Warner, 1994). This

and senior grades on top of across-the-board pay raises to all military
personnel. Thus, the theory predicted that such targeting would result
in greater effort incentives in the military for two reasons. First, the
targeted raises increase the rewards to effort. Second, because
retention increases, individuals have a higher probability of realizing
future rewards to effort, assuming the service does not contract
promotion probabilities by as much as retention increases.

Use of Deferred Compensation Is Expensive When the Discount Rate Is High

The effects of career incentives depend highly on how workers
discount their future earnings. The option of receiving $100 today is
not the same as the option of receiving $100 one year from now. For
example, workers can invest $100 today and obtain more than $100 in a
year. In other words, if a worker has a high discount rate, he should be
offered much more than $100 in the future as a substitute for $100
today.

The individual discount rate determines how costly it is to defer
compensation into the future. If an organization faces the same discount
rate as a worker does, it can invest money now and give the individual
greater rewards in the future. In reality, an individual's discount rate
is often much higher than the organization's discount rate. Available
studies of the individual discount rate in the military estimate it to
be in the range from zero to 30 percent and vary with education, age,
race, sex, number of dependents, ability test score, and the size of
payment (Warner and Pleeter, 2001). Therefore, young workers value a
dollar of the future pension much less than it costs the government or
firm to provide. A firm that maximizes profits cannot offer a worker
more than he is worth over the career; therefore, the larger the
difference between a firm's interest rate and a worker's discount rate,
the less compelling the career incentives are to the worker.

The difference in the firm's and workers' discount rates makes
pension an expensive reward alternative. When workers make decisions
about effort, the possibilities of pensions are in the future. To make a

---

index provides a qualitative indication of the extent to which skewed
pay creates incentives for effort; it does not measure effort directly.

difference in a worker's decision, a pension option should be higher than the corresponding payment in the current period. In this case, it would be beneficial for an organization to decrease wages that are far in the future while increasing current rewards. The higher initial pay can increase the quality of current personnel, while still providing incentives through pensions in the future.

Use of Deferred Compensation Requires Voluntary or Mandatory Separation

Efficient functioning of career incentives requires rules that govern efficient separation of workers. If compensation is deferred, a worker at the end of his or her career is paid more relative to productivity. Therefore, the worker has no incentive to leave the organization at the most efficient point in time. However, an organization cannot afford to pay a senior worker more than he or she had been underpaid in the beginning of the career. Therefore, the organization needs a mechanism to separate workers at some point in time. One suggestion is mandatory retirement that separates them at some predetermined time (Lazear, 1979). The timing of this separation should be such that the total compensation that each worker receives over his or her career is equal to the individual's contribution to the production process.[28] Alternatively, retirement decisions are strongly influenced by Social Security, resulting in voluntary retirement. The existence of a social pension system may obviate the need for the firm to have a mandatory retirement age.

In the military, retirement pay facilitates voluntary separation of service members who reach 20 years of service. In a hierarchical organization, the longer senior workers remain in a job, the slower the promotion rates for younger employees. The retirement system may help to manage the process. When facing the option of receiving a pension, a service member compares his or her rewards from staying in the

---

[28] Although organizations might benefit in some ways from terminating the contract early in the career, so that workers would be underpaid, organizations can earn a bad reputation for reneging on pay or treating employees poorly, thereby hurting their ability to hire high-performing workers in the future. If hiring high-quality employees is important, the organization has an incentive to refrain from such behavior.

organization with the benefits of enjoying retirement. A large enough
pension ensures that personnel will choose to separate from the
organization. This helps the military to keep open the channels for the
advancement of personnel in lower grades. The success of this policy,
however, depends on how well the induced retirement age is selected.

DEFERRED PAY SYSTEMS' POSSIBLE UNINTENDED OUTCOMES

The literature recognizes several effects of the deferred pay
system on the behavior of workers. First, career incentives may induce
young workers to perform too hard. Young workers would like to work hard
to be able to change the perception of the market about their skills.
Second, administrative requirements of the deferred compensation system
may induce undesirable patterns of separation of workers. For example,
the military compensation system may induce some service members not to
separate until they are eligible for retirement pay. The report explains
these effects next.

Deferred Compensation Has the Strongest Effects on Young Workers

The literature suggests that when pay is deferred, junior workers
tend to work too hard while senior workers have incentives to reduce
effort. When workers join firms, little is known about their
performance, so their productivity affects the perception of their
ability. Holmstrom (1982) suggests that junior workers will exert
relatively greater effort when young to change the market's perception
about their quality and performance because they have many years left to
gather returns from their reputations. Therefore, the compensation
system may be structured to support career concerns that are prevalent
among young workers. In particular, greater effort and performance can
be rewarded by faster pay growth.

However, senior workers have less incentive to work as hard because
the market already knows about their productivity, and they have
relatively few years of working left before retirement. Considering this
effect, Gibbons and Murphy (1992) explain that an optimal incentive
scheme involves a heavy reliance on career concerns and salary schemes
for junior and midcareer workers but a weak reliance on career concerns
for senior workers. Moreover, for senior workers, the optimal scheme

should rely heavily on explicit pay-for-performance incentive schemes because career concerns are less relevant.

The Retirement System May Create Undesirable Patterns of Separation

Researchers suggest that the military retirement system may induce undesirable patterns of separation of personnel. First, as described by Asch and Warner (1994a), the system appears to create demand for a large number of midcareer personnel. After a certain point, the promise of pensions is attractive enough to induce workers to stay. However, the military cannot use involuntary separation because it would be considered unfair and would make the services less appealing as a career choice. As a result, the military retains workers who would not be retained under different conditions. Note that a member who does not reach E-6 by 20 years of service must leave the service, which means that the prospect of receiving retirement pay induces an E-5 who may be a mediocre performer and who has little leadership potential to stay in the military for the full 20 years.

Second, the retirement system is identical for all active duty personnel regardless of occupation or service. However, the occupations are likely to require different experience profiles. For example, in combat areas, the military is likely to require a more youthful force. Other military occupations, such as doctors and nurses, could reap returns from extensive training for longer careers. However, as suggested by Asch and Warner (1994a) and Asch, Hosek, and Martin (2002), the experience profiles between occupations are quite similar. The current rules seem to generate a rigid career path and encourage all members of the service to retire after 20 years in service, even though some of them could work productively beyond that period. Therefore, the military could benefit from a more flexible retirement system that encourages workers in some occupations to stay longer.[29]

---

[29] Several alternatives for changing the personnel system are outlined in Asch, Johnson, and Warner (1998). They suggest early vesting of pensions, selective separation bonuses, and eligibility to receive retirement pay not after retirement but later at some predetermined age (i.e., at 62 years) as possible tools to improve flexibility of the retirement system.

Finally, another disadvantage of the current military retirement system is that it tends to separate many workers early in a career (Asch, Johnson, and Warner, 1998). If the services might need to retain workers longer, changes to the retirement system might be necessary.

RELEVANCE OF CAREER INCENTIVES TO MILITARY TRANSFORMATION

Career Incentive Schemes Explain Many Elements in the Military's System of Incentives

This section describes how the model of career incentive schemes complements and accentuates the effects of the tournament system (Section 2). Some of the rewards in the military are deferred. Service members decide how hard to work based on how their pay evolves over their careers. For example, in the case of the promotion system, good performance today is rewarded through increased pay in the future; service members would like to invest early in their reputations and work hard to sustain them. The same holds for retirement pay—an increased stay in the organization is rewarded through a pension once 20 years of service is reached.

The military has several ways to affect the strength of incentives in this system. It can determine how much of the rewards are deferred, which is the degree to which the pay increment from promotion increases with the rank. With respect to retirement pay, the military can choose the size of the retirement package, when retirement is vested, and when service members are eligible to receive benefits.

How Can the Paradigm Support the Objectives of Military Transformation?

Lessons from the career incentive schemes, as applied to the military compensation system, suggest several elements that may not support the goals of transformed military. First, strong reliance on retirement pay may constrain risk-taking and induce conformism in midcareer personnel. Service members would like to play it safe to ensure that they will stay in the military until they are eligible for retirement. However, these effects might be mitigated if performance metrics would reward for innovatory activities and well-calculated risk-taking. As a result, service members would like to develop a reputation consistent with new measures.

Furthermore, the current structure of retirement pay limits the flexibility of the personnel management system. It strongly affects the behavior of personnel by inducing premature separation of some workers and the extended stay of other individuals. These patterns of behavior are not compatible with the goals of transformation. Therefore, any structural changes to the military compensation system should be accompanied by changes to retirement policies.

Some changes have been suggested to allow more flexibility in the retirement system (Asch and Hosek, 2004; Asch, Johnson, and Warner, 1998). For example, a system in which pay is vested earlier but the service members are eligible to receive pay later will provide change to introduce more variability into the system and allow for more variable career length, longer time in assignments, and more variation in time in grade, and, hence, in grade progression. All these changes should weight the current system's benefits against the costs that it might impose on achieving the goals of transformation.

4. EXPLICIT PAY-FOR-PERFORMANCE INCENTIVE MECHANISMS

As described in the previous sections, the current military
compensation system does not fully support the goals of the military
transformation. The major concerns are that the compensation system
might not provide enough flexibility to react to changes in the
requirements for personnel and that the system does not place enough
value on innovation, intelligent risk-taking, and entrepreneurship.
Furthermore, personnel managers need to have more flexible and
innovative ways to use and manage personnel. The most radical approach
to achieve these goals of transformation is to implement a pay-for-
performance compensation system. However, this system cannot be easily
implemented in the military, due to difficulties in measuring relevant
outcomes, multiple dimensions of performance, and role of team effort
when individual performance is hard to measure. Many lessons derived
from this model are important when thinking about efforts of military
transformation. This section reviews the theory of pay-for-performance
compensation schemes, outlines why these models are attractive,
identifies possible costs and unintended outcomes of paying for
performance, and evaluates how different parts of the model can support
military transformation objectives.[30]

PAY FOR PERFORMANCE

Pay for performance ties rewards directly to metrics of
organizational, workgroup, and/or individual performance.[31] These
measures of performance can be linked to base salary, a periodical
bonus, or an incentive pay. This system can be considered a two-part
contract that consists of a fixed salary that does not vary with level
of effort and a piece rate that awards compensation proportionally with

---

[30] This section parallels the discussion in Asch (2005). She
discusses the application of incentives theory to the compensation in
federal government.

[31] Pay-for-performance schemes can be applied to link a reward to a
specific output, sales target, or subjective goal.

the level of output.[32] In extreme cases, the fixed component is zero, and individual's pay depends directly on the quantity of output, such as the number of customers served or the dollar value of sales. For example, in sales, workers usually receive a predetermined percentage of their sales, and their pay depends directly on the revenue that they produce. If compensation is tied directly to the level of performance, the reward is referred to as a high-powered incentive. If the salary or wages do not vary with output, the incentives are considered low-powered.

Currently, the military compensation system does not rely on pay-for-performance mechanisms. Although the compensation system provides bonuses and special and incentive pays, these pays are provided to groups of people, and they do not really recognize the difference in performance between service members.

PAY-FOR-PERFORMANCE'S ATTRACTION

Economics studies suggest two main features that make pay-for-performance compensation schemes attractive. First, piece-rate schemes provide strong incentives for performance. Workers are eager to work harder if they know that their efforts are rewarded through higher pay. Second, piece rates can ensure that people sort into different jobs based on their abilities and willingness to exert effort. More productive workers are more likely to select a job that pays for output, rather than a job that pays a constant wage without considering individual output.

Piece Rates Create Strong Incentives for Performance

Much of the literature focuses on the incentive effects of piece-rate systems.[33] The literature suggests that people perform better when they are rewarded for their performance. Contracts that tie rewards to output provide stronger effort incentives than a wage that does not vary

---

[32] When pay depends on the quantity of output produced, the pay system is called piece rate. It is a particular type of a pay-for-performance system, where performance metrics are simply the number of pieces produced.

[33] See Lazear (1986), and Lazear and Rosen (1981).

with output. Contingent pay arrangements make workers responsible for their effort decisions, and they have incentives to perform well. An optimal mix between fixed and variable parts of the contract depends on the workers' attitudes toward risk (Stiglitz, 1975). Risk-averse workers dislike variation in their income. Therefore, an optimal scheme will provide a fixed component and a smaller proportion connected to the output. Under such an arrangement, the firm provides workers with some insurance against variations of output, but it sacrifices some of the effort incentives available through rewards for output with no fixed component.

Piece Rates Facilitate Sorting of People into Jobs

In addition to the incentive effect, a pay-for-performance compensation system has a selection effect because a higher piece rate is attractive to better workers. If the firm pays piece rates, workers can obtain wages that are proportional to their output, and they can influence their own wages by working harder. However, when an organization pays a fixed salary, all workers receive wages matched to the average productivity in the firm. This means that high-productivity workers will receive salaries appropriate to levels of productivity lower than their own. Therefore, the prospect of receiving higher rewards induces high-productivity workers to join firms that pay piece rates, while less qualified individuals will tend not to join firms that offer this method of compensation (Lazear, 1986).[34] Note that higher-ability workers are not necessarily the best fit to a job. A person can have high ability but low satisfaction from work effort on a particular task. In this case, the piece rate helps sort workers based on their willingness to exert effort at the job.

---

[34] Lazear (1986, 2000b) suggests that the desire to provide variable pay schedule relates to heterogeneity of the workforce. Because of the sorting effect, firms prefer pay-for-performance methods when workers are very different in their abilities, because they induce workers to self-select into different jobs. Note, however, that the piece rate need not be unity to ensure efficient sorting of people into jobs. Lazear (2000b) showed that efficient sorting of workers into jobs exists when the piece rate is positive and close to zero.

Studies of piece-rate compensation in the private sector support both the incentive and selection effects of pay-for-performance schemes. For example, Lazear (2000a) used the individual-level data to study the effect of a piece-rate payment schedule on the performance of workers who install windshields. The estimates suggest that performance, measured as average output per worker, increased by 44 percent after switching from hourly wage to piece rate. About half of the increase was attributed to the increased effort of existing workers. The other half of the increase in productivity was due to the increased quality of workers that the organization was able to attract and retain. Prendergast (1999) reports that about one-third of the increase in performance associated with piece-rate pay is due to the selection of better workers.

PAY-FOR-PERFORMANCE ADMINISTRATIVE COSTS

A well-functioning pay-for-performance compensation system requires several factors. First, it requires measures or metrics of performance. This is the most important part of any compensation system, and pay for performance in particular. Furthermore, it requires a system of monitoring of the worker. The discussion in this section does not relate to the pay-for-performance system only. Lessons from this literature are relevant for the efforts of connecting the goals of transformation to the incentive system in the military.

The Pay-for-Performance System Requires Good Measures of Performance

Good performance metrics should take into account several factors. First, metrics of performance should provide information about workers' performance. This is known as the "Informativeness Principle" (Holmstrom, 1979). Any measure that reveals how effective workers are in their positions should be included in the compensation contract unless it is redundant. It should capture both effort and ability of the worker.

Second, the measures should be prone to measurement error and external factors. Although simple measures like quantity and sales can be easy to observe, they can bias the measures of the performance resulting from the effects of external factors. For example, the level of sales depends not only on a salesperson's effort but also on the state of the economy. When effects of the random factors are large, a piece-rate schedule creates too much variability of earnings that workers do not like, and piece-rate is a less preferred payment option than a salary (Holmstrom and Milgrom, 1987).

Third, the evaluation measures should be aligned with the organization's goals. Baker (1992) suggests that efficiency of the pay-for-performance contract depends on the correlation between what is measured and the organization's goals. If the relation between the measures and objectives is weak, workers' performance accomplishes little toward the organizational goals.

Furthermore, the measures of performance should take into account the objectives of different principals or stakeholders. In a private firm, numerous managers influence workers. Shareholders, labor unions, and consumer groups may intervene as well. When all these principals have different objectives, high-powered incentives, such as pay for performance, will not work well because workers will favor one principal's objective over the objectives of the others. Although one would suspect that it is better for principals to get together and negotiate a scheme that satisfies their joint interest, this rarely happens because they may not share the same information. Dixit (2002) suggests that the best incentive scheme for a setting with multiple principals is one that weakly links pay with performance for any given activity. The weaker link reduces the incentive to divert effort toward the one principal's goals at the expense of the others.[35]

Finally, the selected measures should provide information about various dimensions of the product. This suggests that measures of performance need not be objective and data driven. Although there might be objective measures for many jobs, evaluation based on these objective measures would provide an incomplete view of how an employee is performing. Purely subjective measures also provide valuable information

---

[35] Dixit (2002) also suggests that if the one principal's objectives conflict with the other principal's objectives, incentives for any given activity should be weak. Otherwise, if the principals' goals are complementary, providing high-powered incentives for the activities would help to achieve all objectives.

about the worker's performance, and sometimes they can be easier to implement. The next sections elaborate on the problems that might arise in the compensation system when measures cannot perfectly capture the worker's performance.

Firms Should Bear the Costs of Monitoring Efforts

Because measuring performance is an important part of the pay-for-performance system, firms using it incur the costs of monitoring workers' effort. For example, enterprises might need to install expensive equipment to measure how well workers perform their duties, or they might need to devote substantial labor to monitoring and evaluating workers' performance. Knoeber and McKee (1991) suggest that profit-maximizing firms should consider the costs of monitoring and compare them to the rewards to the firm that the piece rate provides. If the costs of the monitoring effort are higher than gains in productivity, pay for performance is inefficient compared to the salary system.[36] If monitoring is costly, an organization can choose to measure only the minimum amount of effort and connect it to pay. For example, the firm might measure hours worked, and shift the monitoring on supervisors and foremen who monitor performance indirectly, because they are responsible for getting the work done and keeping on schedule. This should be combined with the minimum floor of acceptable performance and a system that fires individuals who fall below that floor (Lazear, 1986).[37] In

---

[36] Monitoring not only *reveals* the level of workers' effort, but can even *change* the level of effort for some workers. Nagin et al. (2002) suggest that workers react to the perceived level of monitoring. When workers perceive the monitoring level to be high, they are less likely to shirk, and the level of shirking depends on workers' satisfaction levels with their jobs. Similar results can be derived from the simple model while allowing for heterogeneity in workers' attitudes toward employers.

[37] The minimum-performance standards can raise the level of effort if workers perceive a benefit from staying in the organization. However, too-high performance standards can diminish effort if workers perceive a low probability of receiving rewards. In addition, these payment options have greater effect on less able individuals, or individuals who have a high disutility of effort, because they are more likely to be affected by the standard (Lazear, 1995).

the military, opinion from colleagues and subordinates may substitute for constant monitoring.

PAY-FOR-PERFORMANCE SYSTEMS' UNINTENDED OUTCOMES

Unintended consequences can arise in organizations that use pay-for-performance compensation schemes. Most of these outcomes are caused by poorly designed metrics of performance. When measures of performance do not reward all-important dimensions of output, workers have incentives to shift their attention from one dimension to the other. For example, workers may improve quantity at the expense of output of the product. Furthermore, workers may strategically shift effort between time periods. In addition, strong individual incentives for performance may undermine team performance. Finally, use of subjective measures of performance may lead to unexpected behavioral responses.

Workers Can Shift Effort Between Measured and Unmeasured Dimensions of Performance

A serious concern about the pay-for-performance system is that mechanisms that reward some but not all characteristics of the output that are important can lead to unintended consequences.[38] For example, the duty of the mechanics in the military is to repair broken equipment. While the number of repairs is easily measured, the quality of repairs is difficult to measure. If not all dimensions of the work are measured, individuals have an incentive to work harder on those dimensions that are measured, and other dimensions may suffer.[39] Holmstrom and Milgrom (1991) provide a model that helps to take into account multidimensional

---

[38] Evidence from the private sector suggests that even small changes in the pay-for-performance incentive structure can produce serious unintended outcomes. For example, if a compensation scheme penalized surgeons for mortality, they would take only less risky patients (Leventis, 1997). If teachers are rewarded based on the students' tests results, they have incentives to teach to the tests or to undertake other activities that can change test results but are not related to students' ability (Jacob and Levitt, 2003). Prendergast (1999) reviews much of the empirical evidence on this topic.

[39] In the private sector, a pay-for-performance scheme that ties reward not to the dimensions of output but to the profits or revenues takes into account all dimensions of output important to consumers (Lazear, 1986). However, profit sharing may have very weak incentives for individuals when the number of participants in the plan increases.

output. The relationship between dimensions of output should determine the choice of rewards. If rewards are based on the number of repairs, mechanics have an incentive to maximize the number of repairs regardless of the effect on quality. Therefore, if some of the dimensions of the output are not easily observed, an optimal solution might be to provide only low-powered incentives on the more easily observed dimensions.[40]

One way to reduce unintended consequences resulting from the pay-for-performance scheme is to design strategically how jobs are bundled and assigned to workers based on the jobs' characteristics. For the mechanics example above, it is true that some of the tasks are more difficult to perform, and mechanics facing a piece-rate incentive scheme may be inclined to choose tasks that are easy to complete quickly. In this case, it is possible to bundle and give each worker a narrowly defined task. For example, one mechanic can concentrate on repairing communication equipment and another on repairing fuel tanks. Dewatripont, Jewitt, and Tirole (1999) show that strategic job design can reduce problems associated with playing a pay-for-performance system. They found that in public organizations, narrow definition of tasks induces more effort on behalf of workers, because they cannot reallocate their effort in unproductive ways.

Workers May Strategically Shift Effort Between Time Periods

Pay-for-performance schemes that reward workers who meet a preset quota may induce workers to shift their efforts strategically between periods. For example, Courty and Marschke (1997) studied job-training centers operating under the Job Training Partnership Act, which provides bonuses if the center meets a certain standard, measured as the number of trainees who find employment by June 1 of each year. The centers have discretion to decide when the trainees would graduate from the program. Courty and Marschke (1997) found that the training centers would strategically manage graduation of their trainees so that the agency met but did not exceed the quota on June 1. If an agency were close to the

---

[40] When output is multidimensional, a salary system works well if the worker does not value one dimension of output, like quantity, over another, like quality (Lazear, 1995).

quota, it would try to do whatever was possible to achieve it to be eligible for a bonus. However, if the agency had already achieved the quota, it had no incentive to report new workers who had found jobs, but instead had an incentive to wait and report those workers in the new season, because graduation in excess of the quota was not rewarded through any additional bonus. This suggests that measures of performance should not just be connected to one specific number, but also to how the measures evolve over time. For example, metrics of individual performance over a year or two provide better information about productivity than a one-time snapshot.

Strong Individual Incentives Can Undermine Team Performance

Rob and Zemsky (2002) suggest that pay-for-performance schemes may undercut incentives for team members to work together. If individual performance is strongly rewarded, workers will work harder on individual tasks and devote less effort to cooperative ones. On the other hand, by selecting less powerful individual incentives, an organization can induce workers to spend less time on tasks that do not require cooperation, i.e., tasks where the individual's effort can be isolated and measured. However, it is possible to design schemes that reward both individual and team performance. This report discusses them in Section 5.

Subjective Evaluations May Lead to Unexpected Behavioral Responses

In addition to influence activities and favoritism,[41] subjective evaluation may lead managers to give overly positive assessments of workers. MacLeod (2001) suggests that differences between managers' evaluations and workers' self-evaluations might create risk of a conflict in the organization. For example, workers might dislike being put into a category of good performers if they consider themselves very good performers. To prevent this conflict, managers might like to converge all evaluations into two categories—acceptable and unacceptable performance—and only the worst workers are given unacceptable evaluations (MacLeod, 2001). Several empirical studies document evidence

---

[41] See Section 2.

of convergence in evaluations. For example, in 2001, of the employees rated on a one-to-five scale in the federal government, 43 percent were rated outstanding, and only 17 percent got anything less than a four on a five-level scale (Friel, 2003). Empirical analysis of the subjective evaluation systems in the private sector also shows a tendency of ratings to be compressed; this compression is more severe the more important ratings are for setting pay (see review in Prendergast, 1999). Note, however, that the incentives to compress ratings can be limited if managers have financial incentives to provide true evaluations of workers. For example, a manager's pay or promotion opportunities can depend on the department's performance.

LESSONS FROM THE PAY-FOR-PERFORMANCE SYSTEM FOR THE EFFORTS OF TRANSFORMATION

Pay-for-Performance Schemes Are Not Used Widely in the Military

The military does not currently use pay-for-performance mechanisms. The current military compensation system uses bonuses and special and incentives (S&I) pays to induce workers to take hazardous assignments and use important skills. Although these payments help the military to meet its larger goals of attracting, retaining, and developing qualified personnel, they do not immediately reward individual performance. In the future, the military might introduce a pay-for-performance compensation mechanism to make the system more flexible and compatible with the goals of transformation. The remainder of this section examines how the lessons from the pay-for-performance models can be applied to the efforts of military transformation.

Factors That Affect Performance

Pay-for-performance schemes provide probably the most flexible way to create incentives in the organization. The idea behind the pay-for-performance compensation system is that workers perform better if they are compensated for additional effort. Performance and appraisal metrics should determine the pay that the worker receives. However, the system's effectiveness depends on how good the measures of performance are.

Designing sound metrics of performance in the military can be quite costly. First, the military's goals are not monetary, and so it is difficult to quantify the value of the services' activities: providing national security, stopping terrorism, deterring aggression, assisting other nations, preventing or reducing conflicts, and fighting and winning major theater wars. Second, at the individual level, the output is multidimensional so that a service member could concentrate his or her effort on only those dimensions of performance that are measured. Third, measures of readiness are both objective and subjective, making individual output difficult to assess and introducing the possibility of favoritism and influence activities. Fourth, military performance relies heavily on team effort, and it is difficult to assess individual contributions to the team's output. All of these factors limit the use of a pure pay-for-performance system for military war-fighters. However, the system can be beneficial to the military if combined with other means of creating incentives like organizational culture and team-specific training (see Section 6).

The Paradigm Can Support the Objectives of Military Transformation

There are several ways in which pay-for-performance mechanisms can help the military to make the system of incentives more compatible with the efforts of transformation. To bring more flexibility in personnel management, the military might want to reward performance within grades, where meaningful performance measures are available. If more variation in career lengths is required, workers who stay for a longer time in their pay grades should be rewarded for their performance, because incentives from promotions would be decreased. In this case, the military could make pay increases contingent on measures of performance within certain grades. Doing so would require structuring pay to improve effort and self-selection, while not neglecting incentives provided through the other modes of compensation. The issue is to determine how the promotion system and a pay-for-performance system can be merged to provide individual-level incentives for performance in the short run, incentives to stay over the long period, and incentives to self-select into needed occupations. This might be difficult to achieve with the current pay table, because spreads between grades might not be large enough to allow meaningful within-grade pay policies. However, the creation of performance-based bonuses would be a way of addressing this limitation.

In addition, the military could rely on pay-for-performance mechanisms to provide incentives for innovation and well-calculated risk-taking. In this effort, however, one needs to have well-designed metrics of performance to minimize possible negative unintended outcomes associated with the system. If monitoring is costly, an organization can choose to measure only the minimum amount of effort and connect it to pay. Even these weak incentives for performance can ensure effort if they are accompanied by a system that separates poor performers. Minimum-performance floors of acceptable performance and separation of underperformers can achieve that.

5. REWARDING TEAMWORK AND COOPERATION IN THE HIERARCHICAL ORGANIZATION

This report has focused on individual incentives but has noted that strong incentives for individual performance relative to incentives for team performance diminish cooperative efforts between workers. However, production effort in an organization often requires cooperation among employees and work in teams; indeed, teamwork plays an important role in the military. This raises the question of how a hierarchical organization should provide incentives for cooperation and teamwork while also creating individual incentives. This section reviews the available literature on team-based incentives. First, it describes what makes teamwork a valuable part of personnel management. Then, it examines factors that may constrain or facilitate the effective use of team effort in many organizations. Finally, it evaluates what these models suggest for the efforts of military transformation.

TEAMWORK IS AN IMPORTANT PART OF THE PRODUCTION PROCESS

Cooperation and teamwork play an important part in the private sector[42] as well as in the military. Service members exert most of their effort as a part of a team. These teams can unite service members with the same or different skills who are working on a project, which can vary from quite small projects like territory control to a more complex job like a joint military command to achieve victory. Teams also unite service members to pool the risk between them. For example, teams in the military usually have excess capacity in certain skills and capabilities, so that workers can be replaced when accidents or casualties occur. Given the important roles that team effort plays in the military, one should worry about how a compensation system could provide incentives for team performance without impeding the individual efforts.

---

[42] Banker et al. (1996) provide a brief overview of the types of teams that can be spotted in the private sector.

There Is No Single Best Approach to Rewarding Teamwork

The available literature suggests that there is no single best approach for rewarding teamwork. However, a combination of models can be used effectively. One possibility for encouraging cooperation in teams is to tie compensation explicitly to group output so that all team members get a reward if some measure of group performance is met. In the private sector, group performance is rewarded through profit sharing and partnership agreements (Gaynor and Pauly, 1990), or through bonus-penalty schemes for teammates (Holmstrom, 1982). Team members share revenues or profits and have incentives to work harder to maximize their shares.

Another approach seems to suggest the use of implicit incentives that are not pay related. For example, implicit incentives may include the following:

- o An individual's motivation to advance his or her career
- o Intrinsic motivation (to care for sick people, for example, or serve the country)
- o Peer pressure and mutual monitoring
- o A corporate culture of hard work and success
- o The motivation high-productivity workers feel to join a team because of the social status they can experience as part of the team

PROBLEMS WITH TEAM INCENTIVES

Although cooperation and teamwork have value in a variety of work settings,[43] several factors can diminish the effectiveness of team-based work settings. First, teamwork is difficult to achieve through individual incentives. Workers who are subject to individual incentives are less likely to help others and cooperate with them. Second, purely team-based incentives might not reward the most able teammates. It is difficult to measure the effect of individual performance on the team's output; therefore, the best performers in the team are rewarded the same way as other teammates. Furthermore, team-based incentive schedules may

---

[43] For example, Boning, Ichniowski, and Shaw (2001) estimated that introducing incentives for team effort increased productivity in U.S. steel mills 0.13 to 0.39 percent, which corresponds to a fiscal benefit of $1.4 million per year.

encourage free riding. When individual effort is hard to determine, some members of the team might opt to reduce their efforts.

Team Effort Is Difficult to Achieve Through Individual Incentives

As mentioned throughout this report, it is difficult to achieve team effort through strong individual incentives. It is hard to determine the contribution of each member to team production, so it is not easy to establish individual incentives for the performance of each worker. In fact, strong individual incentives may limit teamwork and cooperation (Rob and Zemsky, 2002). For example, strong promotion incentives may induce competition between workers and constrain cooperative effort (see Section 2). The evidence supports the view that cooperative effort is much lower in organizations that provide strong incentives for individual performance. This effect is offset by the increase in individual performance under strong individual incentive schemes (Drago and Garvey, 1998).[44] Although individual incentives in the military are strong, performance in teams is also rewarded because subjective evaluations determine how well service members perform in teams.

Team-Based Incentives Do Not Reward the Most Able Workers

Researchers suggest that team-based incentives do not reward the most able workers. If team-based incentives are introduced in place of individual incentives, the performance of more able workers should be expected to decline. These workers have lower rewards from additional effort, because under team performance, the pay depends on the average performance of the group, and additional effort by one worker is shared among all team members. Empirical studies of the performance in the private sector support this hypothesis. Weiss (1988) analyzed data on

---

[44] Drago and Garvey (1998) suggest that reported helping efforts in Australian firms (measured as instances of providing advice about technological processes or allowing the use of tools) are lower in firms that use strong incentive pay in the form of either pay for performance or promotion pay. However, this article suggests only the existence of a correlation between the pay system and cooperation, and it does not examine the causes of why cooperation exists. It seems likely that different jobs require different levels of help and advice, and these jobs can be associated with particular compensation systems.

three plans operated by a large electronics manufacturer. Pay of all new
workers initially depended on their individual productivity. After some
time, workers were moved to a team-based incentive plan, and Weiss
measured the change in individual output. He found that performance of
those who were less productive on the individual pay schemes increased,
while performance of those who were more productive decreased. Hansen
(1997) found a similar result using data on telephone operators. To
qualify for the team bonus, the units needed to achieve a minimum level
of performance. Therefore, the less productive workers were willing to
work harder to enable their teams to qualify for the team-based
incentive payment.

Introducing team performance pay can also affect workers' decisions
to remain in a given organization. Weiss (1988) estimated that, after
the introduction of team incentives, medium-productivity workers are
more likely to remain in the firm than either more able workers or less
able workers. The most able leave because they prefer individually based
incentives elsewhere, where they can make more money, while the least
able leave because they do not like the pressure they feel from their
teammates. There is, however, some evidence that high-productivity
workers join firms despite a decline in monetary rewards (Hamilton,
Nickerson, and Owan, 2003).[45] It is suggested that high-ability workers
may get nonpecuniary benefits from working in a team: they are more
likely to have higher status in the organization or are given additional
authority.

Team-Based Incentives May Encourage Free Riding

Another issue with team-based incentives is that they may encourage
free riding. Consider a team of five workers, each of whom receives as
pay a fraction of the revenues produced by the team. If a teammate
starts working twice as hard as before, team revenues can increase by 20
percent, and each of the workers gets the same increase in pay. However,
the increase in pay for the individual who expanded his productivity

---

[45] Hamilton, Nickerson, and Owan (2003) studied how productivity
changed when a garment plant shifted from individual piece-rate to group
piece-rate production. This change increased worker productivity by 14
percent on average.

does not correspond to his or her increase in effort, and he or she has little incentive to increase productivity. Moreover, because the contribution of each individual to team production is difficult to identify or disentangle, the individual workers in teams have incentives to *decrease* their effort relative to that under individual incentives. This is known as the free-riding effect and it is empirically described in several studies (see Prendergast, 1999, for a review).[46]

The evidence about team performance in the military comes from two occupations: Army recruiters and job counselors. At the lowest level, recruiters are organized into stations. Cooperation and teamwork at the station level is the most relevant for recruiters' success. Recruiters are working at attracting individuals to the military by providing information about the range of available occupations and the types of benefits that the military provides. Job counselors are responsible for matching potential recruits to specific occupations. Recruiters as well as job counselors share responsibility for meeting certain goals related to recruiting personnel in their regions, because their incentive systems include both individual and team factors. Available studies suggest that free riding may be a possibility in military teams. For example, Asch and Karoly (1993) found that counselors in larger battalions earned fewer points on average. For example, counselors in battalions with four counselors earned 81.9 points on average, while those in battalions with nine counselors earned 71.1 points. However, these differences in responses can also arise because of the differences in the resources provided to each unit, goals that were set, and local labor market conditions. The recent evidence suggests that factors like peer pressure and the need to pool risks in a team may improve performance and limit free-riding effects (Dertouzos and Garber, 2004).

OVERCOMING THE FREE-RIDING EFFECT

Of all the problems with team incentives, the free-riding effect is perhaps the most significant. As described by Holmstrom (1982), a possible way to avoid free riding in teams is to design a bonus-penalty scheme that specifies a team bonus when specific team objectives are

---

[46] For examples, see Newhouse (1973) and Gaynor and Pauly (1990).

achieved and a team penalty when they are not. In this scheme, workers may find it too expensive to shirk, and an optimal level of effort can be achieved.

Alternatively, the organization can be divided into sub-teams that compete with each other (Marino and Zábojník, 2003). The competition between teams and the possibility of receiving a reward for winning create high-powered incentives that outweigh the possibility of free riding within teams. This type of competition is used to encourage high performance among recruiting stations in the Army, where pay depends not only on individual performance but also on how the battalion has performed compared to other stations' performance (Asch and Karoly, 1993). However, this approach is not impervious to collusion between firms. If communication or signaling between teams is possible, they may tacitly settle on a lower level of effort than if they were in true competition with one another. In addition, if being the best team depends heavily on random factors or on the systematically unbalanced assignment of recruiting goals to different teams, then competition among teams is likely to be less effective.

One way for an organization to discourage free riding and encourage individual effort is to employ a variety of implicit incentives. For example, it can encourage peer pressure and mutual monitoring among team members (Kandel and Lazear, 1992). Peer pressure is usually incorporated into the special norms that each team member obeys. Whenever an individual deviates from the well-established norms, peer pressure could arise. For example, workers might feel peer pressure to perform well all the time, because they feel responsibility toward their groups. This construct is also related to the idea that workers build their reputations. A worker who wants to create a good reputation will want to avoid feeling guilty from shirking and avoid being shamed if other workers see him or her shirking.

Implicit incentives in the military can also come from the need to rely on teammates to watch one's back to avoid being killed. If an individual shirks and is caught, he or she can no longer have confidence that others are looking out for him or her. This suggests not only that loyalty and team spirit are important factors that influence the

behavior of individuals in teams, especially at lower levels like squad
and platoon, where teammates can easily monitor each other, but also
that they may be born from self-interest and a shared threat of danger.

In addition, an organization that can successfully create a
corporate culture of hard work and success can ameliorate the free-
riding issue. Economists have just started to analyze the possible
effects of corporate culture in an organization. The report briefly
discusses these factors in Section 6. Initial theories suggest that a
firm's culture can improve the sorting of people into jobs and provide
performance incentives. However, the magnitude of these effects is
difficult to estimate due to the correlation of these effects with
compensation and personnel policies, as well as due to the difficulty of
objectively defining corporate culture so its effects cannot be
identified apart from other effects.

TEAM INCENTIVES IN THE TRANSFORMED MILITARY

As described earlier in this section, the value of teamwork has
been well established both in the private sector and in the military,
where much of the output requires team effort. Incentives that promote
cooperation and teamwork are both valuable and necessary. One obstacle
to using team incentives in the military is that it is difficult not
only to isolate individual input from that of the team, but also to
judge how the efforts of a small team (e.g., a tank unit, a special
force operation team, a recruiter's battalion, or a team who prepares a
plane for a combat) contribute to the readiness of the larger team
(e.g., a battalion, brigade, or division).

There are several ways in which compensation system can recognize
team performance. Both pay-for-performance schemes and tournament system
rewards can recognize the team performance explicitly. In this case,
performance metrics should be designed to consider both team and
individual output. For example, in the tournament system, subjective
evaluations by managers and teammates may consider whether or not the
service member is a good team player or team leader. This may limit free
riding and prevent shirking.

In addition, the military can induce team performance through the system of implicit rewards. The military differs from other organizations in how it develops teamwork. The military invests a lot of time and training in developing implicit incentives such as team spirit and group loyalty that motivate cooperation and teamwork. Available evidence from the Army suggests that even when pay is low and punishments for deserting are weak, group loyalty can be an important factor in motivating soldiers to fight. Costa and Kahn (2003) suggest that, during the Civil War when companies of soldiers were created from local conscripts and volunteers, strong ties between soldiers decreased the probability of shirking and increased loyalty to the team. It is still true that intense loyalty to a small group of comrades can be the primary motivation for fighting. When soldiers live together for a long time and in close quarters, endangering the group leads to personal guilt and ostracism by the group.

6. INCORPORATING THE EFFECTS OF NONMONETARY FACTORS

Another set of models that can be applied to the compensation and personnel management system in the military recognizes the importance of nonmonetary factors in the system of rewards. Recently, economists have increasingly recognized nonmonetary factors as possible ways to enhance individual and team job performance and sort personnel into jobs. Considering that the changes brought by transformation can touch different aspects of the military life, weighing the effects of nonmonetary factors is very important to understanding fully the effects of a compensation system. This section describes some of these factors, reviews their effects, and highlights the importance of these factors with respect to the efforts of military transformation.

NONMONETARY FACTORS DEFINED

No compensation system occurs in a vacuum. Besides pay itself, other factors are important for the effectiveness of a compensation system. Although nonmonetary in their nature, these factors can have important effects on the functioning of the compensation system. In particular, this section looks at human resources management tools, an organization's culture, an organization's mission and the value of a given profession, and the degree of authority an individual has in an organization. All of these factors play an important role in the military compensation system.

Human Resources Management Tools

An organization can affect the performance of individuals and teams with a variety of policies and tools that build loyalty and allow people to do their best work. Some that have been identified in the literature include the following:[47]
> o extensive screening process for new hires (e.g., to increase the chances that employees have the right skills for their jobs and fit well into the organization)

---

[47] Among the economic studies of the human resources management tools are Ichniowski, Shaw, and Prennushi (1997), Cappelli and Neumark (1999).

- o flexible job assignments and job rotation
- o employment security
- o individual training
- o teamwork training
- o regular meetings to discuss work-related problems
- o profit-sharing
- o regular evaluations of performance.

Military compensation theory already encompasses such factors as the effects of rules that manage the flow of people across the hierarchy, like up-or-out rules and limited lateral entry. However, there is still a need to know more about the joint effects of personnel practices such as training, job assignment and job rotation, and compensation. The theory suggests that these practices can help improve sorting workers into jobs and their performance afterward. This information can improve the effectiveness of the military compensation system by revealing the factors that affect individual incentives to undertake different job assignments and the influence of these incentives on individual effort and on the larger goals of the military compensation system.

Organizational Culture

One of the factors that affect implicit motivation for workers is an organization's culture or the way things are done in a company.[48] The military has a strong culture that reflects the nature of war fighting in the past, the geography of warfare, and the environment in which war fighting has occurred. Furthermore, each of the services has developed its own subculture that is an important part of its specific identity (see Asch and Hosek, 2004, for a brief overview). The culture of the

---

[48] Pettigrew (1979) suggests that an organization develops a shared language, symbols, ideology, beliefs, rituals, and myths that determine an organization's culture. Camerer and Vepsalainen (1988) refer to corporate culture as a set of broad rules that determine actions in a wide variety of situations. Deal and Kennedy (1982) describe corporate culture as the way things are done in a company. They suggest that the values, heroes, and rituals in a company determine the behavior of workers under different conditions. This behavior creates tacit rules that are transferred to future generations of workers. Schein (1992) suggests that corporate culture is a pattern of basic assumptions that a group learned when adapting to the external environment. These assumptions are later taught to new members of the organization.

military and subcultures of each service can provide implicit incentives for performance. When an individual decides to join the military, he or she decides between the services based on how the services differentiate themselves. Once in the service, the military culture defines the service members' rules of behavior, thus improving performance and communications. When deciding what level of effort to exert, an individual follows the relevant cultural rules. Service members would rather follow the examples of existing cultural norms and increase their chances of promotion within the organization.

Organizational Goals

Organizational goals provide yet another source of intrinsic motivation. Just as workers are likely to self-select into an organization based on organizational goals (see Wilson, 1989, pp. 64-48), military recruits appear to select into the services based on their values or a taste for military service. The military provides unique opportunities for individuals to serve their country, as well as to perform challenging and interesting jobs. Service members understand the importance of their effort to the security of the country and are eager to do their best, even when their output is not readily observable.

Authority and Discretion

The final factor that can motivate workers is the amount of power or discretion given to the individual worker. Although the military is an example of an organization with strict subordination between grades, it provides some authority[49] to lower-level managers throughout the organization. Even if members of the services are given orders about what to do, they have some discretion about how to do it. This provides some implicit incentives to the service members, especially for those who value individual authority.

It is worth noting that military personnel have some authority to affect their subordinates' rewards. Although the structure of monetary

---

[49] Authority can be defined as an ability to select actions that affect part of the organization or the organization as a whole (Simon, 1951).

rewards is fixed in advance and the commanders cannot affect
subordinates' cash compensation in the short run, they can affect
subordinates' compensation in the long run, because performance reviews
affect the speed of service members' promotions. Moreover, they have
substantial freedom in awarding public recognition, formal military
awards, and time off the base. This authority can improve management of
the force and increase the productivity of workers.

NONMONETARY FACTORS CAN AFFECT INDIVIDUAL PERFORMANCE

All of the factors mentioned have the ability to affect individual
performance. Next the report describes how nonmonetary factors can
affect individual performance.

Flexible Personnel Practices Can Increase Productivity

Evidence from the private sector indicates that flexible personnel
practices can increase productivity, and that this effect can be
augmented if several complementary policies are used together.[50]
Ichniowski, Shaw, and Prennushi (1997) examined the effects of
innovative human resources practices on employee productivity in the
steel finishing industry. Innovative policies included profit sharing,
pay for performance, flexible job assignments, employment security and
training, and an extensive screening process for new hires. The authors
estimated that adopting some of the practices increased productivity by
2.3 to 3.5 percentage points. Pooling all of the practices together
increased productivity by 6.7 percentage points. Although these effects
seem small, over a 10-year period these practices alone could increase
operating profits by more than $10 million. The authors found that the
practices were more effective when used in combination than when used
individually. Although these practices can be quite expensive, the
evidence supports the argument that work practices should not be
considered in isolation, but rather as part of a coherent system
(Holmstrom and Milgrom, 1994; Milgrom and Roberts, 1995; Kandel and
Lazear, 1992; Baker, Gibbs, and Holmstrom, 1994b).

---

[50] Also see Cappelli and Neumark (1999).

A Strong Organizational Culture Can Motivate Performance

Economists have described four main ways that an organization's culture may be beneficial to the organization.[51] First, the existence of unified language and norms in an organization can decrease marginal and transaction costs associated with poor communication (Crémer, 1993) and provide the firm with a comparative advantage (Hermalin, 2001). Second, a culture that provides broad rules of conduct for a variety of situations minimizes monitoring costs (Camerer and Vepsalainen, 1988). An organization's culture determines which actions will be rewarded through future cooperation, thus setting a domain for acceptable behavior (Kreps, 1990). Third, corporate culture improves the selection of workers into an organization based on the managers' beliefs: only individuals with similar beliefs will join the firm (Van den Steen, 2001). Finally, corporate culture provides implicit motivation because workers who fit an organization and its culture are more likely to be satisfied with their jobs and, therefore, to exert more effort (O'Reilly, Chatman, and Caldwell, 1991). The problem, however, is that it is impossible to test all these hypotheses empirically.

Although organizational culture provides implicit incentives, the question is how these incentives should be associated with the explicit incentives provided through the compensation system. One possibility is to substitute monetary incentives with nonmonetary rewards. For example, if the intrinsic motivation that a culture provides is strong enough, an organization may decrease compensation and save on salary expenses. This, however, might not sound like a realistic strategy for an existing organization because of the difficulties in estimating effects of the culture on performance.

Alternatively, the organizational culture can be used to complement and reinforce the current system of incentives. The main effect of the organizational culture in the military may come from the development of shared standards of acceptable performance. These standards may complement the system of incentives or may accentuate some other dimensions of performance that are important to the organization. In any

---

[51] For a review of how corporate culture is used in economics, see Hermalin (2001) and Bowles (1998).

case, the culture can be seen as a tool of human resource management, and it is up to the firm to consider the benefits and costs of different elements of a culture that it might want to adopt.

An Organization's Mission and Goals Can Help Sort Workers

When workers are motivated by an organization's goals, they can do their jobs well even for low monetary rewards. Volunteers often effectively perform certain jobs that are important for their community, like caring for sick people, despite the absence of monetary rewards. Similar effects of organizational goals on performance can be found in public organizations. People usually come to work for the federal government not because they expect to receive huge monetary rewards, but because they can relate their objectives in life with the goals of the public organization.[52] For example, a biologist may apply for a job in the EPA because he or she wants to influence environmental policy. A high-school graduate might want to become a police officer to help his or her community develop and prosper. Workers who self-selected into the organization may also be more likely to exert a higher level of effort, because they understand the importance of their contribution to the society or local community. However, there may be plenty of cases in which individuals volunteer to serve a nonprofit organization but do not work hard on the job, or their period of hard work does not last long.

Individual Authority and Discretion Might Motivate Performance

Theoretical studies suggest several reasons why authority and discretion given to workers can motivate individual performance. First, workers can receive satisfaction from being involved in the decisionmaking process and from the sense that they are important to the organization's production process. As a result, they would like to work productively at their current positions and do all they can to be promoted further to receive more authority. Second, authority is valuable when it allows workers to develop their own projects and to manage their tasks as they please, which can increase productivity

---

[52] See Light (1999, 2001) for analyses of different factors that are associated with work satisfaction in the public sector.

(Olsen and Torsvik, 2000; De Bijl, 1995). Third, performance can improve because middle-level managers who have authority might also have better information about the production process. These managers can process newly available information better and faster, which gives them opportunities to react to the possible challenges of the external environment (Boot and Thakor, 2003).

Although providing authority to workers can improve performance, several factors should not be overlooked. First, because the worker's preferences are hidden, the firm may need to monitor the worker at least until it is satisfied that the worker can be relied on to exert the authority effectively (Baker, Gibbons, and Murphy, 1999). Second, because an organization has a finite amount of authority, increasing the authority given to one manager decreases the amount of authority available to other managers, which changes their implicit incentives (Zábojník, 2002). At the same time, it is often possible to have shared or overlapping authority in organizations. Third, in a hierarchical organization, top managers usually have the most authority and can overturn the decisions of subordinates. However, managers also know that authority has positive effects on workers' performance and satisfaction, and they do not want to undermine these effects. Therefore, if managers overturn a popular decision made at a lower level, they must compare the effects of exercising their authority with the costs of workers' declining intrinsic motivation (Aghion and Tirole, 1997).

IMPORTANCE OF NONMONETARY FACTORS IN THE TRANSFORMED MILITARY

Nonmonetary Factors Are Important in the Military Compensation System

Nonmonetary factors play an important role in the military system of rewards. Personnel management practices, corporate culture, amount of authority, professionalism, and organizational goals affect the nature of service members' satisfaction and, consequently, performance on the job. Therefore, the role of these factors can be very important in the system of incentives in the transformed military.

How Nonmonetary Factors Can Support the Objectives of Military Transformation

Findings from the literature on nonmonetary rewards can be used to make military compensation compatible with the efforts of transformation. First, organizational culture can affect patterns of acceptable behaviors by personnel. Therefore, developing metrics of performance directed toward innovative activities and risk-taking should be accompanied with developing a culture that supports these activities. The change might involve changing the attitudes of military personnel throughout the ranks, and senior personnel should take a leading role.

Although intrinsic motivation may be costly to develop, it can provide performance incentives in the military. Kandel and Lazear (1992) used the example of a fighter pilot alone on his or her mission. His or her bravery or cowardice is difficult for others to observe. However, the pilot would like to do his or her best because the squadron's safety depends on his or her success. Therefore, the system of training should continue to develop and support the values that the military finds important.

Moreover, effects of the nonmonetary factors should be taken into account when considering changes to the system of rewards in the military. Training, personnel development, organizational values, and value of authority may affect individual performance in the military. These factors should be designed to work together with the system of explicit incentives.

Furthermore, the military might consider the wider use of nonmonetary rewards in the compensation and personnel management system. For example, personnel might be allowed to have more choice in duty and job assignments, career development, and living environment. Moreover, very strong incentives can be provided by the system of quasi-monetary rewards like allowances for housing and health care. However, the evidence about all these effects is still quite limited.

While using nonmonetary rewards in the military, one should consider the possible interaction between explicit and implicit incentives. The literature is not clear on whether explicit and implicit incentives should be used as substitutes or complements. Difficulty in estimating effects of nonmonetary rewards on performance might limit the use of intrinsic motivation as a substitute for monetary rewards. However, implicit motivations might be used to complement and reinforce the explicit system of incentives.

7. CONCLUDING REMARKS

A transformed military requires a compensation system that not only performs well in terms of recruiting, retaining, and developing able service members, but also provides flexibility in managing careers, and induces creative thinking and performance, innovation, and well-calculated risk-taking. However, what the best policy changes or even viable alternatives are is still an open question. This section summarizes lessons from economics theory on how to connect the structure of incentives with the goals of military transformation.

This report surveyed the economics literature on models of compensation and incentives. Four paradigms of personnel compensation attracted our attention. First, the report discussed how incentives are created when pay depends on the promotion to the higher grade. This is the most important model of compensation in the military. Next, it examined how incentives are provided in compensation systems that defer some part of the rewards into the future. This analytical approach to compensation is applicable to the military because performance in the military in the current period is partially rewarded by higher pay in the future through promotions and eventually retirement. It also looked at the benefits and costs of tying pay directly to certain performance metrics. This scheme arguably provides the most flexibility in managing personnel and creates strong incentives for performance. In addition, the report outlined how nonmonetary factors can affect performance and sorting in the organization, and how they should be associated with monetary incentives. Table 7.1 summarizes the main parts of these models.

Table 7.1

Summary of Models of Compensation

Model	Important Administrative Costs	Important Unintended Consequences
Tournament system	Requires system of evaluating workers. Can include subjective and objective measures. Evaluations can be relative. Needs a system that periodically creates vacancies at the higher grades.	Structure of compensation affects how service members can undertake risks. Subjective evaluations may inspire favoritism and influence activities. May undermine teamwork if it is not recognized in the evaluation process.
Career incentive schemes	The pay structure should be skewed, which can be expensive if the individual discount rate is too high. May require a system of voluntary or mandatory separation.	Have too strong effects on young service members, but less effect on older service members. May create undesirable patterns of separation.
Pay for performance	Requires good measures of performance. Performance needs to be monitored in some way.	Effort can be shifted between measures and unmeasured dimensions of performance. Effort can be shifted between time periods. Strong individual incentives can undermine teamwork and cooperation. Subjectivity in evaluations may lead to favoritism, influence activities and grade inflation.
Nonmonetary rewards	Investments into training, developing of joint culture, costs of using personnel management tools, etc.	May be incompatible with the monetary rewards that exist in the organization.

This review provides several lessons for the efforts of military transformation. Although the current system does not support all goals of transformation, it may not require a complete makeover to be able to deliver on these objectives. Changes in the way the current system works may be able to make it more compatible with the goals of transformation. Even within the tournament system, the main framework that can explain the structure of incentives in the military, it is possible to improve the flexibility of managing personnel. The ranks of warrant officers and career tracks in the Army are possible examples of flexible applications of the current personnel management rules.

Some changes to the military compensation system, however, may help achieve increased flexibility of personnel management. The services might find it beneficial to provide different types of incentives in different occupations or to change how service members are compensated within a grade. The occupations are different in costs of measuring performance. Therefore, it is possible to develop compensation policies that vary between occupations. For example, policies that are tailored to broadly defined occupations can be beneficial in many cases. This approach would significantly increase flexibility of personnel management, and can improve incentives for performance. Although this will decrease reliance on the one-size-fits-all system, it is possible that benefits of this approach outweigh the costs of limiting the system that is the same for all occupations.

Structural changes to the military compensation system may also consider effects of retirement pay. Retirement pay strongly affects the incentive structure that prevails in the military. To allow for more flexibility in managing personnel, the system might allow for different vesting schedules as well as different schedules of eligibility for pay (Asch, Johnson, and Warner, 1998).

An alternative approach to structuring the compensation system would be to link pay directly to metrics of performance. This type of system is known as a pay-for-performance compensation mechanism: employees work harder when they know that each additional unit of output is rewarded through higher pay. This approach to compensation is quite flexible and can immediately reward good performance. These mechanisms can improve the incentive structure within grades, provided that performance metrics capture all necessary dimensions of effort. However, the military might not be able to rely solely on this compensation scheme. One of the most important reasons for this is that pay-for-performance mechanisms require good measures of output. When some dimensions of output cannot be measured well (e.g., one can easily determine weapon qualifications but not unit cohesion), a pay-for-performance mechanism induces workers to produce only in those dimensions that are measured at the expense of the unmeasured dimensions. The role of the nonmonetary factors, however, can help mitigate these effects.

Even the current compensation system may be able to provide incentives for innovatory behavior and well-calculated risk-taking. A tournament system can provide strong incentives to perform in the measured dimensions of performance. Changes to what is considered a good performance affects personnel efforts. Therefore, measures of performance should be compatible with the goals of a transformed military.

Most of the changes to the compensation structure to improve incentives for innovations, creative thinking, and risk-taking require developing new metrics of performance that capture the factors that are important for the goals of transformation. New metrics are rarely easy to develop. Factors that contribute to costs of measuring performance include multiplicity of dimensions of performance, multiplicity of principals with conflicting objectives, and large effects of external factors. In addition, these goals should be connected to the goals of the military compensation system; they should be reliable and feasible. All these costs can affect what approach to compensating a person is the best in terms of creating sustainable performance.

More important, performance measures should be designed to minimize possible negative unintended outcomes. The outcomes of greatest concern should include the possibility of strategically shifting effort between different important dimensions of performance, the possibility of substituting effort across time periods, effects on risk-taking, unproductive activities due to subjectivity in evaluations, and effects on team effort. The current military evaluation system may help to minimize some of the problems. Opinions of multiple supervisors may contribute to the evaluations; the reviews evaluate performance over time. However, it is costly to safeguard against each possible unintended outcome. Therefore, when developing a compensation system, one should compare benefits of each element with its possible costs.

In addition, one should not think about only one model that is applicable to military compensation. Considering the large number of reward mechanisms that can be used in the military, multiple combinations of rewards can bring about the desired outcomes. The elements of the compensation system can either complement or conflict with each other. Although it is easy to consider each component separately, it is an art to combine them all together and explore possible interdependencies and influences on the behavior of workers, or in the case of the military, service members. Combinations of factors should be used to support different alternatives. For example, nonmonetary factors should be used to support compensation in achieving objectives of transformation. Personnel management practices, corporate culture, amount of authority, professionalism, and organizational goals affect the nature of worker satisfaction and consequently performance on the job. In this case, monetary incentives should not interfere with incentives for performance and sorting that are provided through implicit factors.

Although the economics literature provides many useful insights into how a compensation system operates, it has some weaknesses. First, with the exception of a few studies, available theoretical literature is not directly applicable to the peculiarities of the military compensation system. The studies either are too narrow in their scope, make simplistically strong assumptions or assertions, or make assumptions not relevant to the military. Second, a lack of empirical studies constrains understanding of whether the theoretical arguments are important determinants of the behavior of workers. Third, few studies look at the systems of rewards as a coherent mechanism, where different methods of inducing performance and sorting interact.

Looking toward the future, the military might benefit from a compensation system that is compatible with the goals of transformation. The system should not only ensure retention (as it did in the past) but also provide flexibility in managing personnel and induce innovatory activities and well-calculated risk-taking. A successful compensation system should achieve all these outcomes at the least cost. The current compensation system can serve as a benchmark for the comparison of how new policies affect performance of the organization. Additional analysis in this project will use existing data and models to simulate the retention and incentive effects of potential changes to the compensation system. All of the factors mentioned in this report should influence the effectiveness of a particular proposal. Costs and benefits of each alternative should be compared, so one can see how each system performs in terms of satisfying broad retention goals and in terms of creating unintended outcomes and the costs of the system.

BIBLIOGRAPHY

Abowd, John M., "Does Performance-Based Managerial Compensation Affect Corporate Performance?" *Industrial and Labor Relations Review*, Vol. 43, No. 3, 1990, pp. 52S—73S.

Aghion, Philippe, and Jean Tirole, "Formal and Real Authority in Organizations," *The Journal of Political Economy*, Vol. 105, No. 1, 1997, pp. 1—29.

Alchian, Armen A., and Harold Demsetz, "Production, Information Costs, and Economic Organization," *The American Economic Review*, Vol. 62, No. 5, 1972, pp. 777—795.

Asch, Beth J., "Do Incentives Matter? The Case of Navy Recruiters," *Industrial and Labor Relations Review*, Vol. 43, No. 3, 1990, pp. 89-106.

——, *Designing Military Pay: Contributions and Implications of the Economics Literature*, Santa Monica, Calif.: RAND Corporation, MR-161-FMP, 1993.

——, "The Economic Complexities of Incentive Reforms," in Robert Klitgaard and Paul C. Light, eds., *High-Performance Government: Structure, Leadership, Incentives*, Santa Monica, Calif.: RAND Corporation, MG-256-PRGS, 2005, pp. 309-342.

Asch, Beth J., and James R. Hosek, "Military Compensation Trends and Policy Options," Santa Monica, Calif.: RAND Corporation, RB-7533, 2000.

——, *Air Force Compensation: Considering Some Options for Change*, Santa Monica, Calif.: RAND Corporation, MR-1566-1-AF, 2002.

——, *Looking to the Future: What Does Transformation Mean for Military Manpower and Personnel Policy?* Santa Monica, Calif.: RAND Corporation, OP-108-OSD, 2004.

Asch, Beth J., James R. Hosek, Jeremy Arkes, C. Christine Fair, Jennifer Sharp, and Mark Totten, *Military Recruiting and Retention After the Fiscal Year 2000 Military Pay Legislation*, Santa Monica, Calif.: RAND Corporation, MR-1532-OSD, 2002.

Asch, Beth J., James R. Hosek, and Craig W. Martin, *A Look at Cash Compensation for Active Duty Military Personnel*, Santa Monica, Calif.: RAND Corporation, MR-1492-OSD, 2002.

Asch, Beth J., James R. Hosek, and John T. Warner, *An Analysis of Pay for Enlisted Personnel*, Santa Monica, Calif.: RAND Corporation, DB-344-OSD, 2001.

Asch, Beth J., Richard Johnson, and John T. Warner, *Reforming the Military Retirement System*, Santa Monica, Calif.: RAND Corporation, MR-748-OSD, 1998.

Asch, Beth J., and Lynn A. Karoly, *The Role of the Job Counselor in the Enlistment Process*, Santa Monica, Calif.: RAND Corporation, MR-315-P&R, 1993.

Asch, Beth J., and John T. Warner, *A Policy Analysis of Alternative Military Retirement Systems*, Santa Monica, Calif.: RAND Corporation, MR-465-OSD, 1994a.

——, *A Theory of Military Compensation and Personnel Policy*, Santa Monica, Calif.: RAND Corporation, MR-439-OSD, 1994b.

——, *An Examination of the Effects of Voluntary Separation Incentives*, Santa Monica, Calif.: RAND Corporation, MR-859-OSD, 2001a.

——, "A Theory of Compensation and Personnel Policy in Hierarchical Organizations with Application to the United States Military," *Journal of Labor Economics*, Vol. 19, No. 3, 2001b, pp. 523–562.

Auriol, Emmanuelle, Guido Friebel, and Lambros Pechlivanos, "Career Concerns in Teams," *Journal of Labor Economics*, Vol. 20, No. 2, 2002, pp. 289–307.

Baker, George P., "Incentive Contracts and Performance Measurement," *The Journal of Political Economy*, Vol. 100, No. 3, 1992, pp. 598–614.

Baker, George, Robert Gibbons, and Kevin J. Murphy, "Subjective Performance Measures in Optimal Incentive Contracts," *The Quarterly Journal of Economics*, Vol. 109, No. 4, 1994, pp. 1125–1156.

——, "Informal Authority in Organizations," *Journal of Law, Economics, and Organization*, Vol. 15, No. 1, 1999, pp. 56–73.

Baker, George, Michael Gibbs, and Bengt Holmstrom, "The Internal Economics of the Firm: Evidence from Personnel Data," *The Quarterly Journal of Economics*, Vol. 109, No. 4, 1994a, pp. 881–919.

——, "The Wage Policy of a Firm," *The Quarterly Journal of Economics*, Vol. 109, No. 4, 1994b, pp. 921–955.

Baker, George, and Bengt Holmstrom, "Internal Labor Markets: Too Many Theories, Too Few Facts," *The American Economic Review*, Vol. 85, No. 2, 1995, pp. 255–259.

Baker, George P., Michael C. Jensen, and Kevin J. Murphy, "Compensation and Incentives: Practice vs. Theory," *The Journal of Finance*, Vol. 43, No. 3, 1988, pp. 593–616.

Banker, Rajiv D., Joy M. Field, Roger G. Schroeder, and Kingshuk K. Sinha, "Impact of Work Teams on Manufacturing Performance: A Longitudinal Field Study," *The Academy of Management Journal*, Vol. 39, No. 4, 1996, pp. 867—890.

Baron, James N., Alison Davis-Blake, and William T. Bielby, "The Structure of Opportunity: How Promotion Ladders Vary Within and Among Organizations," *Administrative Science Quarterly*, Vol. 31, No. 2, 1986, pp. 248-273.

Bartel, Ann P., "Productivity Gains from the Implementation of Employee Training Programs," *Industrial Relations*, Vol. 33, No. 4, 1994, p. 523.

Becker, Brian E., and Mark A. Huselid, "The Incentive Effects of Tournament Compensation Systems," *Administrative Science Quarterly*, Vol. 37, No. 2, 1992, pp. 336—350.

Boning, Brent, Casey Ichniowski, and Kathryn Shaw, "Opportunity Counts: Teams and the Effectiveness of Production Incentives," Cambridge, Mass.: National Bureau of Economic Research (NBER), Working Paper Series No. 8306, 2001.

Boot, Arnoud W.A., and Anjan V. Thakor, "The Economic Value of Flexibility When There Is Disagreement," Tinbergen Institute, discussion paper no. 2003-002/2, 2003. Online at http://ssrn.com/abstract=367562 (as of March 17, 2005).

Bowles, Samuel, "Endogenous Preferences: The Cultural Consequences of Markets and Other Economic Institutions," *Journal of Economic Literature*, Vol. 36, 1998, pp. 75—111.

Brown, Keith C., W. V. Harlow, and Laura T. Starks, "Of Tournaments and Temptations: An Analysis of Managerial Incentives in the Mutual Fund Industry," *The Journal of Finance*, Vol. 51, No. 1, 1996, pp. 85—110.

Camerer, Colin, and Ari Vepsalainen, "The Economic Efficiency of Corporate Culture," *Strategic Management Journal*, Vol. 9, Special Issue: Strategy Content Research, 1988, pp. 115—126.

Cappelli, Peter, and David Neumark, "Do 'High Performance' Work Practices Improve Establishment-Level Outcomes?" Cambridge, Mass.: National Bureau of Economic Research (NBER), Working Paper Series, No. 7374, 1999.

——, "External Job Churning and Internal Job Flexibility," Cambridge, Mass.: National Bureau of Economic Research (NBER), Working Paper Series No. 8111, 2001.

Carmichael, Lorne, "Firm-Specific Human Capital and Promotion Ladders," *The Bell Journal of Economics*, Vol. 14, No. 1, 1983, pp. 251—258.

——, "Incentives in Academics: Why Is There Tenure?" *The Journal of Political Economy*, Vol. 96, No. 3, 1988, pp. 453—472.

Carmichael, H. Lorne, and W. Bentley MacLeod, "Worker Cooperation and the Ratchet Effect," *Journal of Labor Economics*, Vol. 18, No. 1, 2000, pp. 1—19.

Che, Yeon-Koo, and Seung-Weon Yoo, "Optimal Incentives for Teams," *The American Economic Review*, Vol. 91, No. 3, 2001, pp. 525—541.

Chen, Kong-Pin, "Sabotage in Promotion Tournaments," *Journal of Law Economics and Organization*, Vol. 19, No. 1., 2003, pp. 119—140.

Collins, Joseph J., and T. O. Jacobs, "Trust in the Military Profession," in Lloyd J. Matthews, ed., *The Future of the Army Profession*, Boston, Mass.: McGraw-Hill, 2002, pp. 39—58.

Costa, Dora L., and Matthew E. Kahn, "Cowards and Heroes: Group Loyalty in the American Civil War," *The Quarterly Journal of Economics*, Vol. 118, No. 2, 2003, pp. 519—548.

Courty, Pascal, and Gerald Marschke, "Measuring Government Performance: Lessons from a Federal Job-Training Program," *The American Economic Review*, Vol. 87, No. 2, 1997, pp. 383—388.

Crémer, Jacques, "Corporate Culture and Shared Knowledge," *Industrial and Corporate Change*, Vol. 2, No. 3, 1993, pp. 351—386.

De Bijl, Paul W.J., "Strategic Delegation of Responsibility in Competing Firms," Center for Economic Research, Tilburg University, discussion paper no. 9533, 1995.

Deal, Terrence E., and Allan A. Kennedy, *Corporate Cultures: The Rites and Rituals of Corporate Life*, Reading, MA: Addison-Wesley, 1982.

Department of Defense, Office of the Secretary of Defense, *Military Compensation Background Papers*, Fifth Ed., 1996.

——, *Report of the Seventh Quadrennial Review of Military Compensation*, 1992.

——, *Report of the Ninth Quadrennial Review of Military Compensation*, Washington, D.C., 2002a. Online at http://www.defense.gov/prhome/qrmc/ (as of February 18, 2004).

——, "'Secretary Rumsfeld Speaks on 21st Century' Transformation of the U.S. Armed Forces (Remarks as Prepared for Delivery)," January 31, 2002b. Online at http://www.dod.mil/speeches/2002/s20020131-secdef2.html (as of December 20, 2004).

Dertouzos, James N., and Steven Garber, "Human Resource Management and Army Recruiting: Analysis of Policy Options," unpublished RAND Corporation research, 2004.

Dewatripont, Mathias, Ian Jewitt, and Jean Tirole, "The Economics of Career Concerns, Part II: Application to Missions and Accountability of Government Agencies," *The Review of Economic Studies*, Vol. 66, No. 1, 1999, pp. 199–217.

Dixit, Avinash, "Incentives and Organizations in the Public Sector: An Interpretative Review," *The Journal of Human Resources*, Vol. 37, No. 4, 2002, pp. 696–727.

DoD. See Department of Defense.

Drago, Robert, and Gerald T. Garvey, "Incentives for Helping on the Job: Theory and Evidence," *Journal of Labor Economics*, Vol. 16, No. 1, 1998, pp. 1–25.

Ehrenberg, Ronald G., and Michael L. Bognanno, "Do Tournaments Have Incentive Effects?" *The Journal of Political Economy*, Vol. 98, No. 6, 1990a, pp. 1307–1324.

——, "The Incentive Effects of Tournaments Revisited: Evidence from the European PGA Tour," *Industrial and Labor Relations Review*, Vol. 43, No. 3, 1990b, pp. 74–88.

Fairburn, James A., and James M. Malcomson, "Performance, Promotion, and the Peter Principle," *The Review of Economic Studies*, Vol. 68, No. 1, 2001, pp. 45–66.

Fama, Eugene F., "Agency Problems and the Theory of the Firm," *The Journal of Political Economy*, Vol. 88, No. 2, 1980, pp. 288–307.

——, "Time, Salary, and Incentive Payoffs in Labor Contracts," *Journal of Labor Economics*, Vol. 9, No. 1, January 1991, pp. 25–44.

Faria, João Ricardo, "An Economic Analysis of the Peter and Dilbert Principles," unpublished manuscript, University of Technology, Sydney, Australia, 2000.

Fernandez, Richard L., *The Warrant Officer Ranks: Adding Flexibility to Military Personnel Management*, Washington, D.C.: Congressional Budget Office, February 2002.

Friedberg, Leora, and Anthony Webb, "Retirement and the Evolution of Pension Structure," Cambridge, Mass.: National Bureau of Economic Research (NBER), Working Paper No. 9999, 2003.

Friel, Brian, "The Rating Game," *Government Executive*, August 15, 2003. Online at http://www.govexec.com/features/0803/0803s4.htm (as of August 30, 2003).

Garamone, Jim, "New Act Seeks Flexibility in Military Personnel Decisions," *American Forces Information Service News Articles*, Washington, D.C., April 22, 2003a. Online at http://www.defenselink.mil/news/Apr2003/n04222003_200304221.html (as of December 20, 2004).

———, "Building a First-Rate Personnel System," *American Forces Information Service News Articles*, Washington, D.C., July 18, 2003b. Online at http://www.defenselink.mil/news/Jul2003/n07182003_200307184.html (as of December 20, 2004).

Gaynor, Martin, and Mark V. Pauly, "Compensation and Productive Efficiency in Partnerships: Evidence from Medical Group Practice," *The Journal of Political Economy*, Vol. 98, No. 3, 1990, pp. 544–573.

Gibbons, Robert, and Kevin J. Murphy, "Relative Performance Evaluation for Chief Executive Officers," *Industrial and Labor Relations Review*, Vol. 43, No. 3, 1990, pp. 30–51.

———, "Optimal Incentive Contracts in the Presence of Career Concerns: Theory and Evidence," *The Journal of Political Economy*, Vol. 100, No. 3, 1992, pp. 468–505.

Gibbs, Michael, and Wallace E. Hendricks, "Are Administrative Pay Systems a Veil? Evidence from Within-Firm Data," 1995. Online at http://ssrn.com/abstract=473 (as of March 17, 2005).

Gibbs, Michael, Kenneth A. Merchant, Wim A. Van der Stede, and Mark E. Vargus, "Causes and Effects of Subjectivity in Incentives," 2002, working paper version of forthcoming article. Online at http://ssrn.com/abstract=297744 (as of March 17, 2005).

Green, Jerry R., and Nancy L. Stokey, "A Comparison of Tournaments and Contracts," *The Journal of Political Economy*, Vol. 91, No. 3, 1983, pp. 349–364.

Grossman, Sanford J., and Oliver D. Hart, "An Analysis of the Principal-Agent Problem," *Econometrica*, Vol. 51, No. 1, 1983, pp. 7–46.

Guasch, J. Luis, and Andrew Weiss, "Wages as Sorting Mechanisms in Competitive Markets with Asymmetric Information: A Theory of Testing," *The Review of Economic Studies*, Vol. 47, No. 4, 1980, pp. 653–664.

———, "Self-Selection in the Labor Market," *The American Economic Review*, Vol. 71, No. 3, 1981, pp. 275–284.

Hamilton, Barton H., Jack A. Nickerson, and Hideo Owan, "Team Incentives and Worker Heterogeneity: An Empirical Analysis of Teams on Productivity and Participation," *The Journal of Political Economy*, Vol. 111, No. 3, 2003, pp. 465–497.

Hansen, Daniel G. "Worker Performance and Group Incentives: A Case Study," *Industrial and Labor Relations Review*, Vol. 51, No. 1, 1997, pp. 37–49.

Hermalin, Benjamin E., "Economics and Corporate Culture," in Susan Cartwright, Cary L. Cooper, and P. Christopher Earley, eds., *The International Handbook of Organizational Culture and Climate*, Chichester, England, and New York: John Wiley & Sons, 2001, pp. 217-262.

Holmstrom, Bengt, "Moral Hazard and Observability," *The Bell Journal of Economics*, Vol. 10, No. 1, 1979, pp. 74–91.

——, "Moral Hazard in Teams," *The Bell Journal of Economics*, Vol. 13, No. 2, 1982, pp. 324–340.

Holmstrom, Bengt, and Paul Milgrom, "Aggregation and Linearity in the Provision of Intertemporal Incentives," *Econometrica*, Vol. 55, No. 2, 1987, pp. 303–328.

——, "Multitask Principal–Agent Analyses: Incentive Contracts, Asset Ownership, and Job Design," *Journal of Law, Economics, and Organization*, Vol. 7, Special Issue, 1991, pp. 24–52.

——, "The Firm as an Incentive System," *The American Economic Review*, Vol. 84, No. 4, 1994, pp. 972–991.

Hosek, James R., and Michael G. Mattock, *Learning About Quality: How the Quality of Military Personnel Is Revealed over Time*, Santa Monica, Calif.: RAND Corporation, MR-1593-OSD, 2003.

Hosek, James R., and Jennifer Sharp, *Keeping Military Pay Competitive: The Outlook for Civilian Wage Growth and Its Consequence*, Santa Monica, Calif.: RAND Corporation, IP-205-A, 2001.

Ichniowski, Casey, Kathryn Shaw, and Giovanna Prennushi, "The Effects of Human Resource Management Practices on Productivity: A Study of Steel Finishing Lines," *The American Economic Review*, Vol. 87, No. 3, 1997, pp. 291–313.

Ittner, Christopher D., David F. Larcker, and Marshall W. Meyer, "Subjectivity and the Weighting of Performance Measures: Evidence from a Balanced Scorecard," working paper version of forthcoming article, 2003. Online at http://ssrn.com/abstract=395241 (as of March 17, 2005).

Jacob, Brian A., and Steven D. Levitt, "Rotten Apples: An Investigation of the Prevalence and Predictors of Teacher Cheating," *Quarterly Journal of Economics*, Vol. 118, No. 3, 2003, pp. 843–877.

Junor, Laura, and Jessica S. Oi, *A New Approach for Modeling Ship Readiness*, Alexandria, Va.: Center for Naval Analyses, CRM 95-239, 1996.

Kahn, Charles, and Gur Huberman, "Two-Sided Uncertainty and 'Up-or-Out' Contracts," *Journal of Labor Economics*, Vol. 6, No. 4, 1988, pp. 423—444.

Kandel, Eugene, and Edward P. Lazear, "Peer Pressure and Partnerships," *The Journal of Political Economy*, Vol. 100, No. 4, 1992, pp. 801—817.

Kavanagh, Jennifer, *Determinants of Productivity for Military Personnel: A Review of Findings on the Contribution of Experience, Training, and Aptitude to Military Performance*, Santa Monica, Calif.: RAND Corporation, TR-193-OSD, 2005.

Kilburn, M. Rebecca, and Jacob Alex Klerman, *Enlistment Decisions in the 1990s: Evidence from Individual-Level Data*, Santa Monica, Calif.: RAND Corporation, MR-944-OSD/A, 1999.

Klerman, Jacob Alex, "Measuring Performance," in Robert Klitgaard and Paul C. Light, eds., *High Performance Government: Structure, Leadership, Incentives*, Santa Monica, Calif.: RAND Corporation, 2005, MG-256-PRGS, pp. 343—380.

Knoeber, Charles R., and A. James McKee, Jr., "Accounting Choice: The Role of Monitoring Costs," *Managerial and Decision Economics*, Vol. 12, No. 5, 1991, pp. 353—360.

Knoeber, Charles R., and Walter N. Thurman, "Testing the Theory of Tournaments: An Empirical Analysis of Broiler Production," *Journal of Labor Economics*, Vol. 12, No. 2, 1994, pp. 155—179.

Kotlikoff, Laurence, and Jagadeesh Gokhale, "Estimating a Firm's Age-Productivity Profile Using Present Value of Workers' Earnings," *The Quarterly Journal of Economics*, Vol. 107, No. 4, 1992, pp. 1215—1242.

Kreps, David, "Corporate Culture and Economic Theory," in James E. Alt and Kenneth A. Shepsle, eds., *Perspectives on Positive Political Economy*, Cambridge, England, and New York: Cambridge University Press, 1990, pp. 90—143.

Lazear, Edward P., "Why Is There Mandatory Retirement?" *Journal of Political Economy*, Vol. 87, No. 6, 1979, pp. 1261—1284.

——, "Agency, Earnings Profiles, Productivity, and Hours Restrictions," *The American Economic Review*, Vol. 71, No. 4, 1981, pp. 606—620.

——, "Incentive Effects of Pensions," in David A. Wise, ed., *Pensions, Labor, and Individual Choice*, Chicago: University of Chicago Press, 1985, pp. 253—282.

——, "Salaries and Piece Rates," *Journal of Business*, Vol. 59, No. 3, 1986, pp. 405–431.

——, "Pay Equality and Industrial Politics," *The Journal of Political Economy*, Vol. 97, No. 3, 1989, pp. 561-580.

——, *Personnel Economics*, Cambridge, Mass.: MIT Press, 1995.

——, "Performance Pay and Productivity," *The American Economic Review*, Vol. 90, No. 5, 2000a, pp. 1346–1361.

——, "The Power of Incentives," *The American Economic Review*, Vol. 90, No. 2, 2000b, pp. 410–414.

——, "The Peter Principle: Promotions and Declining Productivity," Cambridge, Mass.: National Bureau of Economic Research (NBER), Working Paper No. 8094, 2001.

Lazear, Edward P., and Robert L. Moore, "Incentives, Productivity, and Labor Contracts," *The Quarterly Journal of Economics*, Vol. 99, No. 2, 1984, pp. 275–296.

Lazear, Edward P., and Sherwin Rosen, "Rank-Order Tournaments as Optimal Labor Contracts," *The Journal of Political Economy*, Vol. 89, No. 5, 1981, pp. 841–864.

Leonard, Jonathan S., "Executive Pay and Firm Performance," *Industrial and Labor Relations Review*, Vol. 43, No. 3, 1990, pp. 13–29.

Leventis, Andrew, "Cardiac Surgeons Under the Knife: A Patient Selection Hypothesis," Center for Economic Policy Studies Working Paper, Princeton University, 1997.

Light, Paul C., *The New Public Service*, Washington, D.C.: Brookings Institution Press, 1999.

——, "To Restore and Renew," *Government Executive*, November 1, 2001. Online at http://www.govexec.com/features/1101/1101plight.htm (as of March 17, 2005).

MacLeod, William Bentley, "On Optimal Contracting with Subjective Evaluation," USC CLEO Research Paper No. C01-8 and USC Law and Economics Research Paper No. 01-11, 2001. Online at http://ssrn.com/abstract=276122 as of March 8, 2005.

Main, Brian G. M., Charles A. O'Reilly III, and James Wade, "Top Executive Pay: Tournament or Teamwork?" *Journal of Labor Economics*, Vol. 11, No. 4, 1993, pp. 606–628.

Malcomson, James M., "Work Incentives, Hierarchy, and Internal Labor Markets," *The Journal of Political Economy*, Vol. 92, No. 3, 1984, pp. 486–507.

Marino, Anthony M., and Ján Zábojník, "Internal Competition for Corporate Resources and Incentives in Teams," working paper version of forthcoming article, 2003. Online at http://www-rcf.usc.edu/~amarino/ as of March 7, 2005.

Medoff, James L., and Katharine G. Abraham, "Are Those Paid More Really More Productive? The Case of Experience," *The Journal of Human Resources*, Vol. 16, No. 2, 1981, pp. 186–216.

——, "Experience, Performance, and Earnings," *The Quarterly Journal of Economics*, Vol. 95, No. 4, 1980, pp. 703–736.

Milgrom, Paul, "Employment Contracts, Influence Activities, and Efficient Organization Design," *The Journal of Political Economy*, Vol. 96, No. 1, 1988, pp. 42–60.

Milgrom, Paul, and John Roberts, "An Economic Approach to Influence Activities in Organizations," *The American Journal of Sociology*, Vol. 94, Supplement: Organizations and Institutions: Sociological and Economic Approaches to the Analysis of Social Structure, 1988, pp. S154–S179.

——, *Economics, Organization and Management*, New Jersey: Prentice Hall, 1992.

——, "Complementarities and Fit: Strategy, Structure and Organizational Change in Manufacturing," *Journal of Accounting and Economics*, Vol. 19, No. 2–3, 1995, pp. 179–208.

Mookherjee, Dilip, "Optimal Incentive Schemes with Many Agents," *The Review of Economic Studies*, Vol. 51, No. 3, 1984, pp. 433–446.

Nagin, Daniel S., James B. Rebitzer, Seth Sanders, and Lowell J. Taylor, "Monitoring, Motivation and Management: The Determinants of Opportunistic Behavior in a Field Experiment," *The American Economic Review*, Vol. 92, No. 4, 2002, pp. 850–873.

Newhouse, Joseph P., "The Economics of Group Practice," *The Journal of Human Resources*, Vol. 8, No. 1, 1973, pp. 37–56.

Oken, Carole, and Beth J. Asch, *Encouraging Recruiter Achievement: A Recent History of Military Recruiter Incentive Programs*, Santa Monica, Calif.: RAND Corporation, MR-845-OSD/A, 1997.

Olsen, Trond E., and Gaute Torsvik, "Discretion and Incentives in Organizations," *Journal of Labor Economics*, Vol. 18, No. 3, 2000, pp. 377–404.

O'Reilly, Charles A. III, Jennifer Chatman, and David F. Caldwell, "People and Organizational Culture: A Profile Comparison Approach to Assessing Person-Organization Fit," *The Academy of Management Journal*, Vol. 34, No. 3, 1991, pp. 487–516.

Ortega, Jaime, "Power in the Firm and Managerial Career Concerns," *Journal of Economics and Management Strategy*, Vol. 12, No. 1, 2003, pp. 1—29.

Orvis, Bruce R., Michael T. Childress, and J. Michael Polich, *Effect of Personnel Quality on the Performance of Patriot Air Defense System Operators*, Santa Monica, Calif.: RAND Corporation, R-3901-A, 1992.

Pettigrew, Andrew M., "On Studying Organizational Cultures," *Administrative Science Quarterly*, Vol. 24, No. 4, 1979, pp. 570—581.

Polich, J. Michael, James N. Dertouzos, and S. James Press, *The Enlistment Bonus Experiment*, Santa Monica, Calif.: RAND Corporation, R-3353-FMP, 1986.

Prendergast, Canice J., "A Theory of Responsibility in Organizations," *Journal of Labor Economics*, Vol. 13, No. 3, 1995, pp. 387—400.

——, "The Provision of Incentives in Firms," *Journal of Economic Literature*, Vol. 37, No. 1, 1999, pp. 7—63.

——, "What Trade-Off of Risk and Incentives?" *The American Economic Review*, Vol. 90, No. 2, 2000, pp. 421—425.

——, "Uncertainty and Incentives," *Journal of Labor Economics*, Vol. 20, No. 2, 2002, pp. 115—137.

Prendergast, Canice J., and Robert H. Topel, "Favoritism in Organizations," *The Journal of Political Economy*, Vol. 104, No. 5, 1996, pp. 958—978.

Risher, Howard, *Pay for Performance: A Guide for Federal Managers*, Washington, D.C.: IBM Center for the Business of Government, 2004.

Rob, Rafael, and Peter Zemsky, "Social Capital, Corporate Culture, and Incentive Intensity," *The RAND Journal of Economics*, Vol. 33, No. 2, 2002, pp. 243—257.

Robbert, Albert A., Brent Keltner, Kenneth J. Reynolds, Mark D. Spranca, Beth A. Benjamin, *Differentiation in Military Human Resource Management*, MR-838-OSD, Santa Monica, Calif.: RAND Corporation, 1997.

Rosen, Sherwin, "Authority, Control, and the Distribution of Earnings," *The Bell Journal of Economics*, Vol. 13, No. 2, 1982, pp. 311—323.

——, "Prizes and Incentives in Elimination Tournaments," *The American Economic Review*, Vol. 76, No. 4, 1986, pp. 701—715.

Salop, Joanne, and Steven Salop, "Self-Selection and Turnover in the Labor Market," *The Quarterly Journal of Economics*, Vol. 90, No. 4, 1976, pp. 619—627.

Schein, Edgar H., *Organizational Culture and Leadership*, 2nd ed., San Francisco: Jossey Bass, 1992.

Scribner, Barry L., D. Alton Smith, Robert Baldwin, Robert L. Phillips, "Are Smart Tankers Better? AFQT and Military Productivity," *Armed Forces and Society*, Vol. 12, No. 2, 1986, pp. 193–206.

Shapiro, Carl, and Joseph E. Stiglitz, "Equilibrium Unemployment as a Worker Discipline Device," *The American Economic Review*, Vol. 74, No. 3, 1984, pp. 433–444.

Simon, Herbert A., "A Formal Theory of the Employment Relationship," *Econometrica*, Vol. 19, No. 3, 1951, pp. 293–305.

Stiglitz, Joseph E., "Incentives, Risk, and Information: Notes Towards a Theory of Hierarchy," *The Bell Journal of Economics*, Vol. 6., No. 2, 1975, pp. 552–579.

United States Code, Title 29, Chapter 18, Employee Retirement Income Security Program, January 5, 1999.

Van den Steen, Eric, "Organizational Beliefs and Managerial Vision," MIT Sloan Working Paper No. 4224-01, 2001. Online at http://ssrn.com/abstract=278200 (as of March 17, 2005).

Ward, Michael P., and Hong W. Tan, *The Retention of High Quality Personnel in the U.S. Armed Forces*, Santa Monica, Calif.: RAND, R-3117-MIL, 1985.

Warner, John T., and Saul Pleeter, "The Personal Discount Rate: Evidence from Military Downsizing Programs," *American Economic Review*, Vol. 91, No. 1, 2001, pp. 33–53.

Wayland, Bradley A., "The Current Officer Evaluation and Promotion System," *Air and Space Power Chronicles*, 2002. Online at http://www.airpower.maxwell.af.mil/airchronicles/cc/wayland.html (as of March 8, 2005).

Weiss, Andrew, "Incentives and Worker Behavior: Some Evidence" in Haig Nalbantian, ed., *Incentives, Cooperation and Risk Sharing*, New York: Rowman and Littlefield Press, 1988.

Williamson, Stephanie, *A Description of U.S. Enlisted Personnel Promotion Systems*, Santa Monica, Calif.: RAND Corporation, MR-1067-OSD, 1999.

Wilson, James Q., *Bureaucracy: What Government Agencies Do and Why They Do It*, New York: Basic Books, 1989.

Winkler, John D., Judith C. Fernandez, and J. Michael Polich, *Effect of Aptitude on the Performance of Army Communications Operators*, Santa Monica, Calif.: RAND Corporation, R-4143-A, 1992.

Zábojník, Ján, "Centralized and Decentralized Decision Making in Organizations," *Journal of Labor Economics*, Vol. 20, No. 1, 2002, pp. 1–20.